MONEY GRAB

MONEY GRAB

AMERICA'S HISTORIC STRUGGLE
WITH SHARING THE WEALTH

Michael D. Ward

MONEY GRAB

Copyright © 2025 by Michael D. Ward. All rights reserved.

No part of this publication may be reproduced, distributed, or transmitted in any form or by any means, including photocopying, recording, or other electronic or mechanical methods, without the prior written permission of the publisher, except in the case of brief quotations embodied in critical reviews and certain other noncommercial uses permitted by copyright law.

ISBN: 979-8-99928-250-7 (Paperback)
ISBN: 979-8-99928-251-4 (Ebook)
ISBN: 979-8-99928-252-1 (Hardcover)

DEDICATION

I was motivated to write this book out of my despair that there is so much backlash against marginalized communities and efforts to drastically cut funding for programs that are critical to their survival. I dedicate this book to all marginalized communities and to those who are still focused on addressing the centuries of disproportionate treatment of large swaths of our population.

CONTENTS

Dedication vii
Introduction xiii
Chapter 1—European Colonization of the Americas and Caribbean Islands 1
    Caribbean, Central, and South American Colonies 2
    Colonial Development in North America 5
    The Seven Years' War and the 1763 Treaty of Paris 11
    Lead-up to Revolution 13
    The Human Toll of the Colonial Era 15

Chapter 2 – Growth of a New Nation 19
    Revolution 19
    Westward Expansion 21
    U.S. Slavery in the Post-Colonial Era 24
    Civil War 26
    Reconstruction and Jim Crow 29
    Pervasive Discrimination by the Federal Government 34

Chapter 3 – Income and Wealth Disparity 39
    Genesis of Disparities in the U.S. 40
    Mid-Century Narrowing of the Income Gap 43
    Return of Wider Income Disparity 47
    Understanding Wealth Disparity 51

Chapter 4 – Cycles of Poverty and Advantage 55
    The Persistence of Poverty 56
    Generational Advantage 59
    Accounting for Taxes and Transfers 61
    Cultural Barriers to Change 65

Chapter 5 – The Federal Individual Income Tax ... 67
- Government Revenue Before Our Current Income Tax ... 68
- Genesis of Our Current Tax Code (1913-1931) ... 73
- Expansion of the Tax Base (1932-1963) ... 77
- Rebalancing the Tax Burden (1964 to 1980) ... 80
- The Modern Era of Taxation (1981 to present) ... 82
- Evaluation of the Progressivity of the Tax ... 88
- Other Tax Impacts ... 89
- Individual Income Tax Policy Recommendations ... 91

Chapter 6 – Labor Practices ... 95
- Organized Labor ... 97
- Federal Support for Labor ... 99
- Minimum Wages ... 101
- Labor Policy Recommendations ... 104

Chapter 7 – The Origins and Taxation of Corporations ... 107
- Financial Institutions ... 109
- The Industrial Revolution ... 110
- The Role of Corporations in our Economy ... 113
- The Role of Corporations in Our Society ... 116
- Corporate Taxation ... 122
- Corporate Policy Recommendations ... 128

Chapter 8 – Shared Self-Governance ... 131
- The History of Democracy ... 133
- U.S. Citizenship and Voting ... 134
- Challenges with the Way Forward ... 136

Chapter 9 – Population Health and Well-Being ... 139
- Health in the Early 20th Century ... 141
- Modern American Healthcare ... 142
- Economic Considerations ... 143
- Health Policy Recommendations ... 145

Conclusion ... 147

Bibliography ... 155

About the Author ... 163

INTRODUCTION

In 1934, then-Senator Huey Long, formerly the Governor of Louisiana, launched the *Share Our Wealth* campaign, advocating for wealth redistribution through progressive taxation, wealth caps, and expansive social programs. While some elements were politically controversial, the message resonated with millions. The movement grew to include approximately 7.5 million members across 27,000 *Share Our Wealth Society* clubs nationwide. After Long's assassination in 1935, the movement lost its central leadership. Under Gerald L. K. Smith, it briefly aligned with Father Charles Coughlin and the Union Party in 1936 but quickly faded.[1]

The campaign is nonetheless credited with influencing elements of President Franklin D. Roosevelt's New Deal, which will be discussed in Chapter 3. The New Deal fundamentally transformed the relationship between Americans and the federal government. However, it also institutionalized racial inequality—especially in housing and employment—entrenching disparities that have marginalized Black Americans for decades and created enduring pockets of poverty.

---

[1] https://www.hueylong.com/programs/share-our-wealth.php

Michael D. Ward

The Declaration of Independence articulates the ideals that inspired the founding of the U.S. These ideals guided the nation as it evolved from a slave-holding society that denied rights to all but white men to one that, at least on paper, affords those rights to all.

> *"We hold these truths to be self-evident, that all men are created equal, that they are endowed by their creator with certain unalienable rights, that among these are life, liberty and the pursuit of happiness."*

Some of the colonies that joined in this declaration and subsequent acts to form a government did not treat all men as equals. They believed that the enslaved people they held were property with no rights of their own. Following a disappointing first attempt to form a government with the adoption of the Articles of Confederation, the founders penned the U.S. Constitution in 1787, which was ratified by the requisite number of states by 1789. The preamble to that document, along with the ideals outlined in the Declaration, provides the foundation for the discussion in this book.

> *"We the people of the United States, in order to form a more perfect union, establish justice, insure domestic tranquility, provide for the common defense, promote the general welfare, and secure the blessings of liberty to ourselves and our posterity, do ordain and establish this Constitution for the United States of America."*

The concept of liberty appears in both documents. It serves as a critical anchor for what our nation aspires to, although it will take significantly more time to ensure liberty or justice for all. Our nation has evolved into one with extreme disparities in wealth and incomes that are exacerbated by policy decisions at the federal government level. The concentration of wealth has expanded into an ominous concentration of power that threatens the achievement of our ideals.

Our Congress increasingly reflects this concentration of wealth and power. Its elected members have just passed legislation to make permanent the 2017 tax cuts that disproportionately benefit those with the highest incomes, while enacting spending reductions in health and social safety net programs needed to pay for them. Two strong but opposing forces in our country seem irreconcilable—those who want to share our wealth with the less fortunate and those who do not. The public discourse is complicated by willful ignorance or misunderstanding of the deeply polarizing and discriminatory history of the U.S., in which white European settlers and their descendants displaced Native Americans, often violently, and subjugated enslaved Africans and their offspring for centuries.

I count myself among those who want to see all Americans enjoy a minimum standard of living without worrying about where their next meal will come from, whether they will have a roof over their head, and whether they will have access to medical care if they fall ill. Given the evolution of our nation over the past 250 years with the overt exclusion of Black and Native Americans from full participation in our economy, I also see a moral imperative to ensure that no one is left behind. Although the U.S. is the wealthiest nation on earth and can certainly afford to guarantee those standards, a persistent cadre of Americans fights against such funding and persistently pushes for tax cuts to retain as much wealth as possible. A central premise of this book is that it is unjust for people to live in poverty in a country of immense wealth.

These explosively opposing forces are deeply rooted in our history; therefore, I dedicate the first part of the book to a review of the early history that has shaped who we are as a country today.

The events that shaped our history started in the 15th century when Europeans set out to explore distant lands in pursuit of wealth. The global population then was estimated to have ranged from 350 million to 500 million, with approximately 70 million residing in Europe. Although they represented only 15% to 20% of the world's population, Europeans sought to dominate other parts of the world.

Europeans had been importing goods such as silk, spices, porcelain, and gems from the *Far East* via land-based routes like the *Silk Road*. However, trade involved numerous intermediaries, and the goods were expensive. As their maritime capabilities improved, many European powers sought alternate trade routes to secure goods at a lower cost. The motivation for exploration was commercial, and those who funded the exploration expected to generate profits from the sale of goods they could procure.

While the exploration spanned the world, the colonization did not. In many parts of Asia and North Africa, established economies existed that facilitated trade and commerce. When Europeans first arrived in the Americas and the Caribbean islands, however, they encountered fewer potential trading partners aside from the Aztec and Incan civilizations. Consequently, Europeans replicated some of the agricultural and mining activities they observed the natives performing.

The level of medical awareness at the time was not advanced enough for the European explorers to realize they could carry diseases that would decimate some of the Indigenous populations they would encounter. However, in the Americas and the Caribbean islands, tens of millions of natives would succumb to disease from initial European contact. Of those who survived, many were subjugated and forced into labor in agriculture and mining activities.

The colonial period was marked by often violent conflict between settlers who believed in their entitlement to the territory they were taking and Indigenous people, whom colonizers viewed as inferior. With their culture infused with the righteousness of their cause, the colonists expanded their presence over decades until they had a critical mass and economic value that was worthy of defense by the British in the French and Indian War. Having won that war, the colonists then felt emboldened to withdraw from the empire and joined with the French to fight for their independence.

Following the Revolutionary War and the establishment of a national government, the new nation led by the progeny of white European immigrants would continue to subjugate and displace others in the pursuit of wealth. For most of the first hundred years as a new nation, a significant share of the Southern economy was driven by the labor of enslaved Africans and their enslaved descendants. For most of the second hundred years, although Black Americans had been emancipated from slavery, they were still held back by widespread nationwide discrimination in housing, employment, and public accommodations.

The approach to taxing individual and corporate incomes has had a significant impact on the disparities we see today. The modern tax system's structure began as a platform to tax the wealthy and reduce tariffs that disproportionately affected those with the lowest incomes. Statements by presidents and members of Congress at the time taxes were first enacted made that policy clear. While taxes to fund the government were not targeted at the working poor, additional efforts were needed to address the conditions of poverty impacting the majority of Americans.

Although the federal government established programs to alleviate some of the burdens of poverty in the 1960s, it has not been able to eradicate the conditions that created concentrated, persistent poverty. Through a combination of tax policy, labor law, and economic factors, the nation's expanding wealth since 1980 has primarily been retained by the wealthiest at the expense of the working and middle classes. To fully address the income and wealth disparities in the U.S., changes will also be required in tax policy, labor policy, and democratic participation.

Some policies that were initially established to help overcome poverty are now being neglected, serving to perpetuate it. The minimum wage once enabled a worker to support a family of four at the poverty threshold and now provides less than half of the income required. While programs have been created to supplement earnings in areas such as housing, health, and nutrition, we have made little progress in addressing the root cause of poverty.

As a society committed to the ideal of meritocracy, we must strive to ensure that individuals have an equal opportunity at critical points in their lives for education and experiences that enable them to realize their full potential. Two of the most significant barriers to that opportunity are persistent poverty and societal structures that rob some people of opportunities available to others solely because of their social status or even the color of their skin.

It has taken the U.S. over 200 years since our founding to begin proactively addressing the impact of centuries of discrimination. There has been intense pushback on progress in the past few years, both racially charged and, to the premise of the book, economically motivated. We will deal with both aspects of that pushback later in the book, but I begin with a grounding in the history that underlies our compelling need to right past wrongs in the first place.

1

European Colonization of the Americas and Caribbean Islands

The history that shaped our nation began in the 15th century when the expeditionary activities of European countries led to the colonization of many parts of the non-European world. Indeed, the trajectory of human civilization shifted significantly at the dawn of the Age of Exploration in the late 15th century, when Europeans began setting out on ships in search of alternative trade routes to Asia. The existing land-based routes to Asia from Europe and North Africa, known as the *Silk Road*, had been developed and used for over 1,500 years, although the routes were often perilous and arduous. Europeans had sufficient wealth to build their own paths to markets and acquire the sought-after goods they desired.

This period is also sometimes referred to as the Age of Discovery—the height of a European-centric view of the world that implied that these places and their inhabitants did not exist until Europeans encountered them. The descendants of these Europeans would take leadership in establishing a new nation on the North American continent that they had conquered. As we will see in the coming pages, the colonizing activities led to the death of millions of Native Americans and the subjugation of millions of Africans. The behavior of many who colonized North America was consistent with that of colonizers throughout the world in its disregard for the lives and liberties of others.

This chapter provides a historical overview of the exploration and colonization that took place during the 15th, 16th, and 17th centuries, the war that established control of North America before the American Revolution, and the human toll of these activities. This is essential for understanding the context in which values developed by the people who formed the United States.

Caribbean, Central, and South American Colonies

Europeans began maritime exploration over 500 years ago, driven by the pursuit of wealth, and discovered islands and continents previously unknown to them. Portugal was the first European nation to undertake maritime expeditions to distant continents in the early 15th century when it explored the Atlantic archipelagos and the western coast of Africa. Finding the islands of Madeira, the Azores, and Cape Verde uninhabited, they claimed them for Portugal and established settlements in 1419, 1432, and 1456, respectively. During the rest of the century, they continued south along the western coast of Africa, establishing trading posts. Their exploration advanced south through the Gulf of Guinea, the mouth of the Congo River, and Cape Cross in present-day Namibia. They also began to capture or buy and transport slaves to sugar plantations established on Madeira and the Azores.

Sailing for Spain in 1492, Christopher Columbus discovered several islands in the present-day Bahamas as well as the Islands of Hispaniola and Cuba. He returned to Spain from this expedition with gold and spices, as well as several natives who had been kidnapped from the islands. Pope Alexander VI issued the *Inter Caetera*, a proclamation known as a papal bull, that acknowledged the discovery of distant lands inhabited by others. It asserted that the Spanish monarch had a divine right to those lands and that non-Christian nations should be overthrown and brought to the Catholic faith. This would be used to justify Spain's conquest of numerous Caribbean islands and parts of Central and South America.

The *Inter Caetera* also granted Spain dominion over discoveries to the west of a line in the Atlantic 100 leagues west of the Cape Verde Islands, with Portugal retaining dominion over discoveries east of that line. After some negotiation, Portugal and Spain agreed to a treaty line in 1494 that was slightly further west. This ultimately resulted in Portugal's settlement in present-day Brazil, which fell east of the line, and Spain's dominance in the rest of South and Central America. Because Africa fell entirely on the east side of the line, Portugal led the transatlantic slave trade. No other European nations would abide by these rights granted just to Spain and Portugal.

Spain colonized the islands of Hispaniola, Cuba, and Puerto Rico in 1493, 1508, and 1511, respectively. All the islands were densely populated with Taino and related tribes who were engaged in mining and agriculture. While initial contact in Hispaniola was peaceful, Columbus would return with 1,000 men to establish an outpost just a few years later. Many of the natives succumbed to *Old World* diseases carried by the Spanish explorers, who struggled to find gold on their own and forced the Taino into labor, first on Hispaniola and soon after in Cuba and Puerto Rico. Between disease and exploitation, the Taino would experience a near-collapse of their population. The Spanish colonists turned to the Portuguese, who had already been engaged in the slave trade, to purchase slaves to continue the arduous mining and later agricultural activities, which began when gold deposits were harder to find.

When Spanish explorers, led by Hernán Cortés, arrived in present-day Mexico in 1521, they encountered a more organized resistance from the Aztec Empire but ultimately vanquished it. They then repeated the same pattern of subjugating the natives who survived disease and replacing them with enslaved Africans when their numbers no longer supported the labor requirements of the colonial economy. Exploration ventured south to present-day Guatemala, where they conquered the Mayan Empire, and north to the present-day southwestern U.S. This broad area was known as New Spain.

Portuguese explorer Pedro Álvares Cabral first landed in present-day Brazil in 1500; however, colonization did not begin until the 1530s. Unlike the more structured societies found in Central America, Brazil comprised many smaller tribes dispersed across the region. Still, they numbered between 2 million and 5 million at the time of first contact. They, too, would succumb to disease, and survivors were forced into labor. The Portuguese also brought enslaved Africans to Brazil, which became the largest destination for the Atlantic slave trade.

Spanish and Portuguese colonization in the Caribbean islands and Central and South America resulted in the loss of tens of millions of lives of Indigenous people. It firmly established the Atlantic slave trade that would later extend to colonies in North America. Collectively, more than half of the enslaved Africans transported in the Atlantic slave trade were forced to work in Spanish and Portuguese colonies in the New World.

Colonial Development in North America

The French and English started exploring the eastern coast of North America in the 16th century. They did not establish lasting settlements until the 17th century, when France, England, the Netherlands, and Sweden established the first enduring coastal colonies in North America. This chapter will highlight some early colonies and key milestones to provide insight into the colonial era, which led to a diverse mix of settlements. Like the colonizing activities in other parts of the world described above, violence against Native Americans and other colonies was frequently used to secure a dominant position in the lands claimed by the colonists.

England's King James I chartered two companies in 1606 to explore and colonize North America: the Virginia Company of Plymouth and the Virginia Company of London, clearly establishing the commercial intent behind colonization. Both companies explored and settled parts of North America in 1607. The Plymouth Company's settlement in present-day Maine was abandoned within a year. The London Company's settlement in Jamestown ultimately survived, though conditions in Jamestown were harsh, and many early settlers succumbed to disease.

The colonists began planting tobacco in Jamestown using seeds brought from the Caribbean islands, laying the foundation for an export trade that would fulfill the settlement's commercial objective. They continued to expand their presence and battled with Native Americans for decades until they achieved a dominant position after the Native American population declined due to deaths from disease and war with the colonists.

In 1624, the Dutch established the colony of New Netherland, centered in present-day New York but extending north to Cape Cod and south to the present-day state of Delaware. While early relations with the Native Americans in the area, primarily the Algonquin and Iroquois, were initially peaceful, tensions with the Native Americans escalated as competition for resources increased with the growing number of colonists. Kieft's War from 1643 to 1645 destroyed all sides, and the Peach Tree War of 1655, fomented by Dutch involvement in the settlement of New Sweden, resulted in significant losses among the colonists. The colony became a bustling port and trade hub in the New World; however, at its height, New Netherland had only about 9,000 residents, compared to approximately 80,000 in New England.

The Massachusetts Bay Colony was established in 1630 by a royal charter granted to a group of Puritans. Initial interactions with the local natives, who had been in the territory for hundreds of years, were cooperative, and they engaged in trade. After more settlers arrived over the following several decades, tensions with the natives increased. The Puritans believed they had a divine right to occupy the land, which led to territorial disputes. This all bubbled over with King Philip's War from 1676 to 1677, so named because the English referred to the Wampanoag leader Metacom as King Philip. The brutal war devastated the Native American population, and survivors were largely driven west to accommodate the English victors, who also suffered significant casualties.

To constrain the expansion of the Dutch settlement of New Netherland by England's imperial rivals, King Charles I granted a charter in 1632 to Caecilius Calvert, the 2nd Baron of Baltimore, to settle the lands north of the Virginia colony. The Baron's younger brother, Leonard Calvert, traveled with the settlers in 1634 and led the colony, the Province of Maryland, on his brother's behalf. A trading license previously awarded to a Virginia official to establish a trading post in the Chesapeake Bay area sparked a territorial dispute that would pit Calvert against the Virginia official in a series of incidents spanning 20 years. Imprecise borders and, thus, seemingly overlapping claims would spur war between European colonies throughout the 1600s.

The Maryland settlements encroached on lands occupied by Native Americans, who initially sought trade with the settlers. Some land was purchased from the Native Americans, and several treaties were also negotiated. As with other colonies, settlers brought diseases that spread among the Native Americans and killed many of them. As the English presence in the colony grew over the next several decades, conflict arose with the Native Americans and the Virginia colony to the south. The colonists waged war with the Susquehannock tribe between 1642 and 1652. Most other natives were displaced, moving westward or onto reservations, with those remaining assimilated into the colonial population.

Michael D. Ward

The English and Dutch both explored the Connecticut River valley. In 1633, the Dutch purchased land from the Pequot tribe to establish Fort Hope, a settlement at the mouth of the Connecticut River. English colonists from the Plymouth colony settled in Windsor the same year, while Puritans from the Massachusetts Bay Colony settled in Wethersfield in 1634 and Hartford in 1636. The English settlements came together to form the Connecticut Colony in 1636.

The expansion of the English settlements encroached on Pequot lands. With support from the Mohegan and Narragansett tribes, the English waged war with the Pequot in 1636 and 1637. The war ended with the Mystic Massacre of 1637, where hundreds of Pequot were killed or enslaved. A separate New Haven colony was established in 1638 with strict religious laws, which merged into the Connecticut Colony in 1662 when a royal charter was granted. Connecticut became the first colony to establish its own constitution, the Fundamental Orders of Connecticut, in 1639.

The only Swedish colony in North America was established in 1638 on land along the present-day Delaware and Schuylkill Rivers, which includes parts of present-day New Jersey, Pennsylvania, and Delaware initially claimed by the Dutch. The local Native Americans also contested outside ownership of some of the land. Still, the settlers maintained peaceful relations with the natives, often purchasing land rather than seizing it, as was the custom of many Dutch and English settlers. The Dutch conquered the colony in 1655 and incorporated it into their territory of New Netherland. Many Swedish settlers remained under subsequent Dutch and later British rule.

King Charles II drove the expansion of the colonies by granting three proprietary charters. He ascended to the throne following an interregnum, during which England was governed as a Commonwealth under Oliver Cromwell and, briefly, his son Richard Cromwell. The King recognized the efforts of the eight lords who helped him secure the throne by granting them a charter for the Carolina colony. As with the Virginia colony, the climate favored agricultural activities and natural resources that could be used in shipping. They developed an economy based on tobacco, rice, and naval stores, including pitch, tar, and turpentine. Initial interactions with Native Americans focused on trade, but like other colonies, the continued arrival of European settlers and expansion of the colonial presence resulted in tensions with Native Americans. The Carolina colony was split into North Carolina and South Carolina in 1712, and each received a royal charter in 1729.

Because New Netherland was managed as a business by the Dutch West India Company, the settlers expressed significant frustration over a lack of clear laws and a judicial structure. Accordingly, the Dutch faced a series of economic and governance challenges, and in 1664, they surrendered the New Netherland colony to the English. King Charles II granted the Duke of York a proprietary charter, and the colony was renamed New York. The Dutch colonists largely remained, some moving north to the Albany area.

King Charles II granted William Penn a charter to land west of the Delaware River in what is now present-day Pennsylvania in 1681. Penn settled in the area to maintain religious freedom and live peacefully with the Native Americans. He acquired land through purchase and negotiated treaties. These alliances helped him defend the borders to the north with New York and the south with Maryland. Pennsylvania established its Charter of Privileges in 1701, declaring its own self-governance.

The initial settlers of the Maryland colony were primarily Protestants, though the Calvert family was Catholic and, therefore, placed mostly Catholic leaders in positions of power. A few years after Calvert returned to England to pursue a border dispute with William Penn, the Protestant Revolution of 1689 resulted in a faction taking local control and enacting anti-Catholic ordinances, which led to the cancellation of the Calvert charter. The King sent a series of governors, starting in 1692, to operate as a royal colony. When Charles Calvert and his son Benedict died within a few months of each other in 1715, the King restored the charter to their heir, also named Charles, the 5th Baron of Baltimore, upon his declaration of the Anglican faith and subsequent move to Maryland to lead the colony.

In 1732, King George II granted a charter to a group of 20 trustees, led by James Oglethorpe, to establish and maintain a colony named the Province of Georgia for the benefit of the poor, many of whom were imprisoned for debt. The colony would also serve as a buffer to the Spanish colony in Florida, potentially drawing them into war in 1739 and 1742. Oglethorpe objected to slavery, so the colony was organized around small plots that families could tend to independently, unlike the large plantations in other Southern colonies. He also banned alcoholic beverages. These restrictions led to dissatisfaction by the colonists, who saw the more successful slave-based plantation economies around them. As this was the last colony to be established before the Revolutionary War, it attracted as many settlers from the neighboring colony of Carolina as it did from Great Britain.

Colonial history is critical because it sets the pattern of dispossession that increased in scale and impact as the U.S. expanded westward following its founding, which is described in more detail in Chapter 2. It also showcases the religious, cultural, and economic diversity that developed across the colonies that later joined to form a new nation. At this point in history, however, they had a shared enemy, and unity brought strength.

The Seven Years' War and the 1763 Treaty of Paris

By 1754, all 13 colonies that would later declare independence were under British control, while the French and British vied for supremacy in international trade routes and colonial influence beyond Europe. French colonies in North America spanned from the Mississippi Basin in Louisiana to the continent's center, encompassing the Great Lakes and extending north into present-day Canada. Although three earlier wars between British and French interests in North America were described as the French and Indian War, the fourth and largest French and Indian War began in 1754 when British, French, and Indian forces clashed at Fort Duquesne over control of the Ohio River Valley. Native Americans were drawn into the conflict depending on which side they traded with, as they stood to lose land in the war. This war precipitated and was subsumed into the Seven Years' War that would engulf the globe.

The Seven Years' War, from 1756 to 1763, was the first global war, encompassing North America, Europe, Africa, India, the West Indies, and the Philippines. The European portion of the war primarily pitted Prussia against Austria, with each nation supported by its respective allies. Great Britain was allied with Prussia, while France, Saxony, Spain, Sweden, and Russia were allied with Austria. The British leveraged the European war to tie up the French, who lacked significant naval strength, allowing the British to overwhelm French colonies worldwide.

The French and British also fought short battles over territory in West Africa, the Philippines, India, and several Caribbean islands. The war in India erupted following a longstanding conflict between the British East India Company and the French East India Company to gain control of the Indian Subcontinent. Indian allies of the trading companies were drawn into the war, which raged for several years and ended with a British victory. The African war included successful British incursions on French settlements in Senegal and the Gambia. The war in the West Indies included the British invasion of Guadeloupe, Martinique, Cuba, and the Bahamas.

When Spain's King Ferdinand VI died in 1759, Carlos III, who was related to French King Louis XV, succeeded him. Their relationship led to the Family Compact between France and Spain, in which Spain began actively supporting France in the Seven Years' War. This cooperation included an embargo on British goods, the seizure of British goods, and the expulsion of British merchants from Spain. In retaliation, the British declared war on Spain in 1762, bringing them into the Seven Years' War.

The French quietly negotiated the Treaty of Fontainebleau in 1762 to secure Spain's support for the exchanges needed to settle the Seven Years' War. France gave Spain the Louisiana Territory west of the Mississippi River in exchange for support in the negotiations to end the Seven Years' War. This side agreement was unknown to the other parties to the 1763 Treaty of Paris, which reflected that the Louisiana Territory would remain under French control. The transfer to Spain wasn't made public until 1764, and Spain didn't fully take control of the territory until 1769.

The 1763 Treaty of Paris negotiated a settlement of hostilities among Great Britain, France, and Spain. The French were willing to cede New France in present-day Canada but did not want to relinquish the islands, so they offered the French territory east of the Mississippi River, up to and including present-day Canada, in exchange for the return of Guadeloupe and Martinique. The British accepted the exchange because the territory east of the Mississippi River served as a buffer for their coastal colonies and an opportunity for future expansion. Spain ceded Florida to the British, allowing the British to gain control of North America east of the Mississippi River. Though the French ceded a fair amount in the settlement of the war, they would later join the British colonies in North America in fighting for freedom from Great Britain.

Lead-up to Revolution

Following the Seven Years' War, Great Britain was on the verge of bankruptcy with a significant debt load. The colonies were also feeling an economic pinch, having lost the flow of silver and gold paid by Great Britain for provisions for the military engaged in the war. Nonetheless, the colonies benefited from the war, and the British believed it was reasonable to impose taxes on the colonies to help repay the debt. Parliament passed the Sugar Act in 1764, imposing a tax on the import of foreign goods, and the Stamp Act in 1765, which assessed a tax on legal documents, academic degrees, newspapers, pamphlets, and other printed materials.

Colonial merchants paid excise taxes on sugar and molasses while boycotting certain imports and smuggling other goods to evade the tax. The Stamp Act had a more profound impact on colonists, leading to a more significant resistance movement. Nine colonies convened a Stamp Act Congress that successfully petitioned the British Parliament to repeal the act. The British then imposed import duties on British china, glass, lead, paint, and paper under the Townshend Acts in 1767. This further angered the colonies, precipitating more protests and increased tensions. The colonists' frustration overflowed when Parliament passed the Tea Act in 1773, which sparked the Boston Tea Party.

The British Crown appointed Thomas Gage to serve as Royal Governor of Massachusetts in 1774 with the direction to quell the unrest. The British Parliament then increased pressure on the colonies by passing a series of acts drafted by Gage, known as the Intolerable Acts—the Boston Port Act, Massachusetts Government Act, Administration of Justice Act, Quartering Act, and Quebec Act. These closed the Port of Boston, restrained self-governance, limited the colonists' ability to try British officials for crimes in the colonies, required colonists to house and feed British soldiers, and expanded the territory of Quebec. The colonies viewed this as a significant overreach by Great Britain, uniting them and prompting calls for a Continental Congress to collaborate on a response.

The Human Toll of the Colonial Era

Before discussing the revolution and the establishment of the new nation in the next chapter, this section provides a recap of how colonists affected others. The demarcation point for historical analysis of the Americas is 1492, when Christopher Columbus first arrived in the region. The history preceding that date is referred to as the pre-Columbian period. The pre-Columbian population of North America, South America, and the Caribbean islands is estimated to have been between 50 million and 100 million. In contrast, the European population at the time was estimated to be between 70 million and 90 million. The Europeans introduced diseases to the New World, for which the native population had no natural immunity, including measles, smallpox, influenza, and bubonic plague, also known as the *Black Death*. Tens of millions of natives were lost to these diseases, with as much as 90% of the pre-Columbian population dying by the end of the 1500s.

Throughout the Caribbean, Spain brutally subjugated the survivors among the native population who did not succumb to disease. They were forced into labor, cultivating sugarcane and other cash crops and mining for gold. Many of these surviving natives subsequently died from the harsh working and living conditions. The plantation economy was lucrative for Spain, though, so African slaves were brought to the islands to continue exploiting the resources with forced labor. Portugal was the first nation to engage in large-scale slave trade in the 1400s and was the primary source of slaves imported into Spanish colonies in the 1500s.

The Indigenous people on Hispaniola suffered greatly. Pope John Paul II acknowledged the complicity of the Catholic Church in a 1992 visit to the Dominican Republic on the 500th anniversary of Columbus' landing there and the ensuing atrocities of conquistadors. Also, during a 2015 speech in Bolivia, Pope Francis spoke more explicitly about the role of the church. "I say this to you with regret: Many grave sins were committed against the native peoples of America in the name of God," he said. "Here I wish to be quite clear, as was St. John Paul II: I humbly ask forgiveness, not only for the offenses of the church herself, but also for crimes committed against the native peoples during the so-called conquest of America."[2]

In 1619, the British captured two Portuguese ships off the coast of the Americas and brought the 20 slaves to Point Comfort near the Jamestown Colony. These slaves were put to work in the tobacco fields. They thus began 200 years of slaves being imported into North America, which initially used indentured servants who traded a period of servitude in exchange for passage to the New World. The plantation economy in the Southern colonies was labor-intensive. It required increasing levels of effort to meet the demand for the cash crops they produced, which plantation owners used as a justification for using enslaved labor.

---

[2] https://www.usccb.org/committees/native-american-affairs

The Dutch East India Company also engaged heavily in the slave trade during the 1600s and 1700s. The trans-Atlantic slave trade during the colonial era violently displaced approximately 12.5 million Africans, who were forced into slavery and sold to European colonists throughout the Americas.[3]

- 1.8 million were estimated not to have survived the passage on slave ships
- 4.8 million were sent to the Portuguese colonies, primarily in Brazil.
- 2.3 million went to the British colonies in the Caribbean.
- 1.1 million were shipped to the French colonies in the Caribbean.
- 1.3 million were delivered to the Spanish colonies in the Caribbean and South and Central America.
- 0.4 million slaves were trafficked to the British colonies in North America.
- Other slaves were trafficked to Dutch and Danish colonies, primarily in the Caribbean.

Once in the colonies, slaves were subjected to torture and physical punishments; overwork and brutal working conditions; separation and dehumanization; sexual, psychological, and emotional abuse; and unsafe living conditions. Slaves were most often put to work in agricultural and household activities in the Southern colonies, which had primarily plantation economies that produced crops such as cotton, rice, and tobacco, as well

---

[3] https://www.slavevoyages.org/assessment/estimates

as other cash crops. Slaves had no control over their lives. Their children were born into slavery and were often sold, tearing families apart.

In addition to the devastation by disease, Native Americans died in wars with each other and with the colonists, as there was significant pressure to yield land to colonists. Less known is that many Native Americans were also forced into slavery, not just on the continent but often sold to slavers who transported them to the Caribbean islands, where they were working other slaves to death, and the labor-intensive sugar plantations needed more laborers. This practice gutted many Native American communities and families.

The colonial period in American history is often told from the standpoint of the settlers, most of whom set out for the New World to pursue new opportunities, more freely express their religious beliefs, and forge a new life. While many settlers were the families and peaceful neighbors of the leaders who engaged in violence to secure the colonial territories, most shared a cultural belief in the superiority of the Europeans and their right to occupy the land they claimed. That cultural foundation was handed down over generations, leading to many white Americans today feeling a sense of entitlement about the country and a disdain for others who challenge their superiority.

Growth of a New Nation

The colonial period culminated with the now-firmly established colonies at odds with the imperial government. Following a brief discussion of the formation of a new country and the war to secure its independence, this chapter will focus on territorial expansion, the institution of slavery, the Civil War, and the subsequent century of institutionalized racial discrimination. This period further ingrained a sense of white superiority and entitlement in American culture and set the stage for deep and enduring poverty among many Black Americans.

Revolution

In the first session of the Continental Congress (referred to in the last chapter), which met in Philadelphia in September 1774, delegates agreed to boycott British goods if Parliament did not repeal the Intolerable Acts and convene a second Congress the following spring if necessary. In April 1775, Governor Gage feared a rebellion was brewing and sought the help of British troops to seize weapons and armaments from the local militia. The colonists learned about the plan and the gathering of troops in Boston. The local militia readied to defend the colony, surprising the British soldiers when they arrived. The Battles of Lexington and Concord marked the beginning of the Revolutionary War, which spanned over eight years. During the Revolutionary War, some Native Americans fought with the British, hoping to limit further incursions into their territories.

The Second Continental Congress met in Philadelphia in May 1775 and agreed to assemble a Continental Army from the militias in each colony under the leadership of George Washington. They also sent an Olive Branch petition to King George III, which the monarch refused to consider, declaring that the colonies were in a state of revolt. The Congress then met again a year later, and on July 4, 1776, the terms of the Declaration of Independence were finalized.

Following the declaration, the war expanded beyond New England to the other colonies. The Continental Congress adopted the Articles of Confederation in November 1777, which served as the first constitution of the U.S. but failed to provide a mechanism for levying taxes or regulating commerce. Ten years later, a new U.S. Constitution was written and signed. It did not take effect until late 1789, after at least nine states had ratified it.

The Revolutionary War is thoroughly covered in numerous other texts, so my purpose here is to highlight it as a milestone in the evolution of the new nation. The U.S. won the war and, in the 1783 Treaty of Paris, was recognized as a free and independent country. The British ceded control of significant territory, including the 13 colonies plus the Northwest Territory, the space between the Mississippi and Ohio rivers south of the Great Lakes. It returned to Spain most of present-day Florida, which it won in the 1763 Treaty of Paris. Following this, the United States expanded primarily through acquisition, forcibly removing and displacing Native Americans in all the territories.

Westward Expansion

Although the U.S. gained control of the Northwest Territory through the 1783 Treaty of Paris, it was slow to occupy the area, which was estimated to be inhabited by approximately 45,000 Native Americans. Several early conflicts were settled with the 1784 Treaty of Fort Stanwix and the 1785 Treaty of Fort McIntosh. The U.S. fought the Northwest Indian War from 1785 until 1795, attempting to wrest control of the region from the many remaining Native American nations that inhabited it. That war was settled with the 1795 Treaty of Greenville.

During the first half of the 19th century, the U.S. paid or negotiated with other European powers to relinquish their claims on land from the Mississippi River to the West Coast and also established the borders between the U.S. and Canada to the north and Mexico to the south. Notably, though tens of millions of dollars were spent, these were not purchases from the Native Americans who inhabited the territories. Their land was often seized, and they were displaced.

The U.S. paid for the French to relinquish claims on approximately 828,000 square miles of land west of the Mississippi River in 1803 through the Louisiana Purchase, effectively doubling the country's territory in North America. Neither the French nor the Spanish had settled much of the territory except around New Orleans. It was primarily inhabited by Native Americans who had never ceded land to any European powers and instead had numerous agreements to coexist and trade with the Europeans. None of these agreements was honored as the U.S. battled and displaced Native Americans as they moved west.

The War of 1812 was fought in the Great Lakes region between the British and allied Native Americans and the U.S. with its own tensions in parts of the Northwest Territory that had yet to be settled by the U.S. This resulted in Tecumseh's War, with the British joining forces with Native Americans in the War of 1812, in which the British fought back against U.S. invasions into the British territories in Upper Canada.

In 1818, the U.S. entered into the Anglo-American Convention, which established the northern border between the U.S. and Britain for portions of North America west of the Mississippi River to the Rocky Mountains along the 49th parallel. It also resulted in the joint occupation of what would become known as the Oregon Territory between the Rocky Mountains and the Pacific Ocean. Spanish and Russian claims to the far western portion of this territory were relinquished in the Adams-Onis Treaty of 1819 and the Russo-American Treaty of 1824, respectively.

The Florida territory changed hands several times between Great Britain and Spain, including as part of the agreements under the 1763 Treaty of Paris, which settled the Seven Years' War, and the 1783 Treaty of Paris, which settled the American Revolution, leaving Florida in Spain's hands. In 1819, the U.S. acquired approximately 72,000 square miles, comprising the

Florida Territory, through the Adams-Onís Treaty, which also clarified the boundary between New Spain and U.S. territories.

In 1845, the U.S. acquired approximately 389,000 square miles when it annexed Texas in exchange for $10 million in debt incurred by Texas during its brief period of independence from Mexico, which had lasted less than 10 years. As with all acquisitions, expansion into these lands would be at a cost to Native Americans.

In 1846, the U.S. secured approximately 280,000 square miles in the Oregon Territory, which it jointly occupied with the British. Through the Oregon Treaty, the British and U.S. continued the northern border on the 49th parallel from the Rocky Mountains to the Pacific Ocean. Though the Spanish and Russian claims to parts of the Oregon Territory had previously been resolved by treaty, the U.S. government forcibly displaced Native Americans to make room for white settlers.

In 1848, the U.S. acquired approximately 525,000 square miles through the Treaty of Guadalupe Hidalgo, which concluded the Mexican-American War. This area encompassed most of the present-day southwestern United States and extended to the West Coast in present-day California. The treaty did not recognize the rights of Native Americans, who were also forcibly removed, enabling white settlers to stake claims on the territory.

Under the Gadsden Purchase in 1853, the U.S. acquired approximately 30,000 square miles, extending the southern border with Mexico along the Rio Grande and the 32nd parallel in present-day Arizona and New Mexico. This was the last land purchase in what would become known as the lower 48 states. As in earlier acquisitions, Native Americans were not considered and were displaced by white settlers.

The westward expansion of the U.S. was not bloodless. Following the Louisiana Purchase, the resettlement of Native Americans from Georgia, the Carolinas, and the Louisiana territory spanned four decades. Some Native American tribes negotiated treaties under which they were granted land in the Indian Territory, now present-day Oklahoma. They included some of the most contentious acts of forced displacement, including the Trail of Tears. For more than 100 years, the effects of displacement and broken treaties continued to work their way through the courts and Congress, culminating in the creation of the Indian Claims Commission in 1946. The Commission negotiated settlements with Native American nations for decades more, the last claim being settled in 2012.

U.S. Slavery in the Post-Colonial Era

Nothing demonstrates the struggle some Americans have had with sharing wealth more than the perpetuation of slavery . By 1776, Black Americans, both free and enslaved, made up approximately 20% of the population. There was much discussion at the Constitutional Convention, with even some slave-holding founders acknowledging that slavery was contrary to their belief in the natural rights of all men. In drafting the U.S. Constitution, they reached a compromise with the Southern states, for which slavery was an essential element of their economies and included a provision in the first clause of Section 9 of Article I:

> "*The migration or importation of such Persons as any of the states now existing shall think proper to admit, shall not be prohibited by the Congress before the year one thousand eight hundred and eight, but a tax or duty may be imposed on such importation, not exceeding ten dollars for each Person.*"

Though the provision expired in 1808, Congress passed the Act Prohibiting the Importation of Slaves in 1807 with an effective date of January 1, 1808. Neither the clause in Section 9 nor the 1807 legislation addressed the abolition of slavery itself, just the importation of slaves. While the U.S. outlawed the importation of slaves, it is estimated that thousands of new slaves were brought into North America through the Spanish colonies in Florida and Texas before their admission to the Union. At this point, several generations of children were born into slavery, and several more generations would be born into slavery in the 19th century.

Tensions between the U.S. states that allowed slavery and those that did not grew throughout the early to mid-1800s as new territories were acquired and states were carved out of them. Missouri was admitted as a slave state through the Missouri Compromise of 1820, which also admitted Maine as a free state. The agreement also established a dividing line between areas of the Louisiana Territory where slavery was legal to the south and where it was illegal to the north.

When territories were acquired from Mexico, the Compromise of 1850 enabled California to join the Union as a free state and created the Utah and New Mexico territories, where the issue of slavery would be decided by settlers in those territories rather than by Congress. Notably, however, the Compromise included the Fugitive Slave Act, requiring citizens to help capture runaway slaves to be returned to their owners, which angered abolitionists in the Northern states and further increased tensions.

The Kansas-Nebraska Act was passed in 1854 to establish those territories, allowing the settlers to decide whether to allow slavery. The abolitionist movement clashed with pro-slavery factions in a conflict known as Bleeding Kansas because this act effectively repealed the Missouri Compromise that limited slavery to territories below the 36th parallel.

In 1857, the U.S. Supreme Court ruled in Dred Scott v. Sandford that enslaved people were not citizens and that Congress could not prohibit slavery under the Constitution. The decision also unconscionably reinforced the position that the Fifth Amendment right to hold property free from government interference protected slaveholders' rights, as slaves were considered property. This fueled pro-slavery sentiment in the Southern states and added urgency to the abolitionist movement. A constitutional amendment would later overturn this disastrous decision.

Civil War

The tension between pro-slavery and abolitionist forces reached a crescendo by 1860 when Abraham Lincoln ran for president of the U.S. on a platform that opposed the expansion of slavery into the western territories destined for statehood. Notably, while he abhorred slavery, he did not campaign to eradicate it but instead to prevent new states and territories from joining the Union as slave states. Southern states nonetheless recognized that slavery as an institution might ultimately fall if the limitation on its expansion were to take hold.

Lincoln was elected on November 6, 1860. Before his inauguration on March 4, 1861, seven states seceded from the Union and began organizing as the Confederate States of America. Within one week of Lincoln's inauguration, the assembly of the Confederate States approved a new Constitution. Unsurprisingly, the Constitution of the Confederate States of America adopted in 1861 at the dawn of the Civil War did embrace slavery and expressly provided that "no law denying or impairing the right of property in negro slaves shall be passed." Thirty days later, the Confederacy started the Civil War by firing on Fort Sumter in South Carolina, where the Union Army was gathering munitions to hold off a rebellion President Lincoln feared would be coming. Within three days of this first attack, Lincoln indeed declared that an insurrection was at hand. In the next few weeks, four more states seceded from the Union.

Lest there be any confusion about the role slavery played in the formation of the Confederacy and the outbreak of the Civil War, Mississippi delegates to the Constitutional Convention, called to secede collectively from the Union, issued A Declaration of the Immediate Causes which Induce and Justify the Secession of the State of Mississippi from the Federal Union, which states, in part, that:

> *"Our position is thoroughly identified with the institution of slavery-- the greatest material interest of the world. Its labor supplies the product which constitutes by far the largest and most important portions of commerce of the earth. These products are peculiar to the climate verging on the tropical regions, and by an imperious law of nature, none but the black race can bear exposure to the tropical sun. These products have become necessities of the world, and a blow at slavery is a blow at commerce and civilization. That blow has been long aimed at the institution, and was at the point of reaching its consummation. There was no choice left us but submission to the mandates of abolition, or a dissolution of the Union, whose principles had been subverted to work out our ruin."*

And in closing:

> *"Utter subjugation awaits us in the Union, if we should consent longer to remain in it. It is not a matter of choice, but of necessity. We must either submit to degradation, and to the loss of property worth four billions of money, or we must secede from the Union framed by our fathers, to secure this as well as every other species of property. For far less cause than this, our fathers separated from the Crown of England."*

The war was brutal, spanning four years and claiming 1.5 million casualties, including 700,000 deaths—the most significant loss of American life of any single war in history. Imagine fighting that hard to retain the legal right to enslave other human beings. Detailed histories of the war are available elsewhere, so the rest of this chapter will instead focus on the period following the war. The war ended when Confederate General Robert E. Lee surrendered to Ulysses S. Grant at Appomattox on April 9, 1865. Abraham Lincoln was assassinated at Ford's Theatre in Washington, D.C., just days later, dying on April 15.

Reconstruction and Jim Crow

Lincoln's vice president, Andrew Johnson, was sworn into office and would lead the period of Reconstruction that began following the end of the Civil War in 1865. The first few years were challenging because he was sympathetic to the Confederacy and undermined the progress of key reforms. The war impoverished the South, which had been heavily dependent on agriculture before the war and lacked significant industrial capacity. The South withheld cotton shipments to Europe early in the war, hoping to draw Europe into the war. It proved to be a substantial miscalculation. Europe began buying cotton from Egypt and India, and the South lost its dominance in the European marketplace, though it could sell some cotton again after the war. The Union Navy's blockade of Southern seaports played a crucial role in ending the war by preventing the South from securing essential supplies or resuming its exports, with lasting effects. Several sectors of Southern states' economies continue to struggle today.

The 13th Amendment to the U.S. Constitution, which banned slavery or involuntary servitude except when a person is duly convicted of a crime, was first drafted in the Senate Judiciary Committee in January 1864 and passed by the full Senate in April 1864. It did not pass in the U.S. House of Representatives when first put to a vote in June 1864 and was only passed when a new House was seated in January 1865, with a very narrow margin. Ratification was completed by December 1865.

To ensure emancipated slaves would have full rights, Congress passed the first Civil Rights Act in early 1866. Notably, Andrew Johnson vetoed the act; however, Congress had a sufficient alignment of purpose that allowed it to override his veto, and the act became law. It said, in part:

> *"Citizens of every race and color... shall have the same right, in every State and Territory in the United States, to make and enforce contracts, to sue, be parties, and give evidence, to inherit, purchase, lease, sell, hold, and convey real and personal property, and to full and equal benefit of all laws and proceedings for the security of person and property, as is enjoyed by white citizens..."*

Johnson's veto foreshadowed his lack of enforcement. The Southern states were resistant to the act's requirements, and without executive action, enforcement was limited. Losing the war did not change the sentiment for the white people in power in the Southern states. They quickly sought ways to suppress and control newly freed Black Americans by enacting *Black Codes* intended to limit the economic, political, and social freedoms of formerly enslaved Black Americans. These laws were explicitly designed to enable continued white exploitation of Black American labor, effectively extending the economic benefit of slavery.

Some of the most egregious laws subjected Black Americans to arrest for petty and contrived offenses, including failure to provide annual written proof of employment. A punishment often available for these arrests was for the state to hire out the arrestees to perform labor without compensation. One law even allowed the state to take children from Black Americans it felt they could not support and then apprentice the children to their former owners for a period of labor without pay.

In June 1866, the 14th Amendment was introduced and passed in the U.S. Congress. This is one of the most consequential amendments because it not only granted birthright citizenship but also recognized a right to due process before any person can be deprived of life, liberty, or property and guaranteed equal protection under the law. It would take two years for it to be ratified, and it went into effect in July 1868.

The continued resistance from the Southern states prompted Congress to pass the Reconstruction Acts of 1867, all of which were vetoed by Johnson but then overridden by Congress. These acts required the states to create new state constitutions, subject to congressional approval, that guaranteed voting rights for all men regardless of race and to ratify the 14th Amendment. These acts also divided the Southern states into five military districts, providing military oversight of the re-registration of voters, including Black men, as well as the reorganization of state governments.

Congress also passed the Tenure of Office Act of 1867, limiting the president's ability to remove federal officials, including Cabinet members, without Senate approval. Johnson was impeached in 1868 for his dismissal of Edwin Stanton, the Secretary of War who was working with Congress to implement the military oversight. Johnson was acquitted in the Senate, so he continued to serve out his term.

The 15th Amendment, passed by Congress in 1869 and ratified in 1870, guaranteed the right to vote regardless of race, color, or previous condition of servitude. Ulysses S. Grant succeeded Johnson as president, serving from 1869 to early 1877. He was a strong supporter of reconstruction efforts and established the federal Department of Justice in 1870, in part to investigate acts of violence against Black Americans.

Under the Black Codes, Black Americans were being denied equal access to public accommodations, so Congress passed the Civil Rights Act of 1875:

> *"All persons within the jurisdiction of the United States shall be entitled to the full and equal enjoyment of the accommodations, advantages, facilities, and privileges of inns, public conveyances on land or water, theaters, and other places of public amusement; subject only to the conditions and limitations established by law, and applicable alike to citizens of every race and color, regardless of any previous condition of servitude."*

In one of the many unfortunate 19th-century U.S. Supreme Court decisions, they struck down this key provision of the 1875 Act. Ruling in 1883 on a series of cases known as the Civil Rights Cases, the majority opinion, written by Justice Joseph Bradley, held that the 14th Amendment barred states from passing discriminatory laws, but it did not enjoin private conduct. He wrote that "it is State action of a particular character that is prohibited. Individual invasion of individual rights is not the subject matter of the amendment." It further enshrined the thinking that held our nation captive for the following eight years:

"It would be running the slavery argument into the ground to make it apply to every act of discrimination which a person may see fit to make as to the guests he will entertain, or as to the people he will take into his coach or cab or car, or admit to his concert or theater, or deal with in other matters of intercourse or business..."[4]

Because neither candidate in the 1876 presidential election received a sufficient number of undisputed Electoral College votes, a divided Congress established an Electoral Commission comprising members from the Senate, the House of Representatives, and the Supreme Court. Disputed slates of electors from Florida, Louisiana, Oregon, and South Carolina were evaluated, and the election was decided in favor of Rutherford Hayes. The final resolution, unofficially known as the Compromise of 1877, led to the withdrawal of federal troops from the Southern states and marked the end of the Reconstruction era.

Racially discriminatory *Jim Crow* laws were then passed that disenfranchised Black Americans, turning back political and economic gains made by them during Reconstruction. These laws imposed segregation in public accommodations, education, and transportation, effectively consigning Black Americans to second-class citizenship by force of law. These laws, which persisted well into the 20th century, created the conditions that resulted in the deep and intractable poverty that generations of Black Americans have experienced. In 1896, the Supreme Court upheld the constitutionality of racial

---

[4] https://constitutioncenter.org/the-constitution/supreme-court-case-library/the-civil-rights-cases

segregation in Plessy v. Ferguson, establishing the "separate but equal" doctrine legitimizing the *Jim Crow* laws.

The racial animus and desire to retain and control wealth ran so deep that all but one of the former Confederate states passed new constitutions, erecting barriers to voting in ostensibly non-racial ways to comply with the 15th Amendment. Literacy tests, property ownership requirements, and poll taxes excluded most Black Americans and many poor white Americans from voting. However, *grandfather laws* in some states were used to allow anyone to vote whose ancestors voted before the Civil War, helping poor white Americans who might be unable to meet the other requirements.

With the suppression of Black American votes, the white Southern Democrats gained control of all Southern state governments. They would systematically underfund education for Black American children and skew the curriculum to glorify the Confederacy and denigrate Black Americans in public education. The governments implemented policies that perpetuated low-wage and exploitative labor conditions for Black Americans while tolerating or participating in racial violence with no justice for the victims. Many also commissioned monuments and public symbols to honor the Confederacy—often decades after the Civil War—as part of a broader effort to reassert white dominance.

Pervasive Discrimination by the Federal Government

The Southern Democrats were able to secure the election of Woodrow Wilson in 1912 and his re-election in 1916.

Despite support from some Black Americans based on anti-discrimination rhetoric in his campaign, Wilson imposed discriminatory hiring practices and racial segregation in federal government workplaces during his first term. Institutionalized discrimination during his presidency negatively impacted Black American federal workers and their families for decades.

The federal government failed to hold states accountable for ensuring protections articulated in the 13th, 14th, and 15th Amendments. Separate but equal accommodations, education, and other areas of life were underfunded, and there was no enforcement. The Department of Justice did not yet have a Civil Rights Division, which was established with the passage of the Civil Rights Act of 1957. Although there was a small Office of Education, it received little emphasis until the creation of the Cabinet-level Department of Health, Education, and Welfare in 1953.

While New Deal programs that Franklin D. Roosevelt launched in the 1930s would provide some benefits to Black Americans, as implemented, they reinforced segregation with discriminatory housing and employment programs. The Fair Labor Standards Act of 1938 exempted certain jobs from its provisions, which were most likely to be held by Black Americans, including farm workers on small farms, domestic service workers, and railroad and motor carrier workers. As Black Americans were struggling to gain a foothold in the economy that had so long excluded them, the exclusion of specific jobs from protections became yet another barrier.

Another instance of uneven progress began to unfold in the housing arena. The Home Owners' Loan Corporation (HOLC) was established in 1933 to refinance mortgages that had defaulted. It also created a housing appraisal system with color-coded maps that characterized the riskiness of loans in various neighborhoods, labeling those deemed hazardous in red, which led to the term *redlining*. Those neighborhoods were almost always disproportionately inhabited by Black Americans.

The National Housing Act of 1934 established the Federal Housing Administration (FHA), which provided mortgage insurance to stimulate the development of new housing. These programs enabled millions of families to enjoy middle-class lifestyles and build wealth. The law granted the Federal Housing Administrator broad discretion to establish regulations, which limited FHA approval to neighborhoods considered lower-risk and excluded primarily Black American communities, as coded in red on the HOLC maps.

An extract of two sections from the FHA underwriting manual from 1938 illustrates how its programs reinforced school segregation and housing discrimination (see item 980(3)g and the third sentence in 982(1) below):

> *"980 (3). Recorded restrictive covenants should strengthen and supplement zoning ordinances and to be really effective should include the provisions listed below. The restrictions should be recorded with the plat, or imposed as a blanket encumbrance against all lots in the subdivision, and should run for a period of at least twenty-five to thirty years. Recommended restrictions should include provision for the following:*
>
>> *a. Allocation of definite areas for specific uses such as single or two-family houses, apartments, and business structures*

b. *The placement of buildings so they will have adequate light and air with assurance of a space of at least ten feet between buildings*
c. *Prohibition of the resubdivision of lots*
d. *Prohibition of the erection of more than one dwelling per lot*
e. *Control of the design of all buildings, by requiring their approval by a qualified committee, and by appropriate cost limitations or minimum square foot ground floor areas*
f. *Prohibition of nuisances or undesirable buildings such as stables, pig pens, temporary dwellings, and high fences*
g. *Prohibition of the occupancy of properties except by the race for which they are intended*
h. *Appropriate provisions for enforcement.*

982 (1). Adequacy of Civic, Social, and Commercial Centers. These elements of comfortable living usually follow rather than precede development. Those centers serving the city or section in which the development is situated should be readily available to its occupants. Schools should be appropriate to the needs of the new community and they should not be attended in large numbers by inharmonious racial groups. Employment centers, preferably diversified in nature, should be at a convenient distance. Source: Federal Housing Administration, Underwriting Manual: Underwriting and Valuation Procedure Under Title II of the National Housing Act With Revisions to February, 1938 (Washington, D.C.), Part II, Section 9, Rating of Location."

The U.S. Supreme Court affirmed the constitutionality of the poll tax, a discriminatory practice in many Southern states, in its 1937 decision in Breedlove v. Suttles.

President Franklin D. Roosevelt issued an executive order in 1941 banning racial discrimination in federal employment and contracting practices, but he never took action to roll back the FHA's discriminatory underwriting rules. The discriminatory programs were finally dismantled in the 1950s and 1960s after having done irreversible damage by creating segregated communities of concentrated poverty. As we will see in the next chapter, it is challenging to climb out of concentrated, institutionalized poverty.

Income and Wealth Disparity

There is a growing yet uninformed view in the U.S. today that society is colorblind, that everyone has equal opportunity, and that everyone should compete based solely on merit. While some individuals may have less conscious bias, it is essential to recognize how income and wealth disparities hinder the full realization of a society with equal opportunities. The centuries of discrimination described in the earlier chapters cause these disparities to impact Black and Native Americans disproportionately.

While income does not always correlate with wealth, it often does. To be sure, it is impossible to build wealth without having disposable income after paying basic living costs. While some people with higher incomes match their consumption to their earnings and fail to save or invest much, that is a choice they have the luxury of making. This chapter will review the origins of our disparities and their evolution since America's founding. The next chapter will discuss the persistence of poverty and the generational transmission of wealth.

Michael D. Ward

Genesis of Disparities in the U.S.

Diversity in income and wealth was present but not extreme at our nation's founding because the scale of domestic commerce in our agrarian economy was mainly local. Arable land was the primary source of wealth, and many founders believed that an equal distribution of land would afford everyone equal opportunity at self-sufficiency and the ability to increase their wealth based on their efforts. Such a distribution of land never occurred, and public lands were sold at prices only the wealthy could afford until the passage of the Homestead Act of 1862 enabled some to receive free land grants in exchange for a pledge to occupy and cultivate the land for a minimum of five years. Wealth did grow, however, from commerce. Millionaires who emerged in the first half of the 19th century gained their wealth from banking, the fur trade, and real estate. International trade was lucrative, and urban centers involved in such trade were robust economies, creating opportunities for wealth creation.

Many Southern plantation owners who built wealth on the backs of enslaved workers also became millionaires. In 1860, Natchez, Mississippi, had the highest percentage of millionaires of any city in the U.S. While these millionaires initially lost significant wealth when their slaves were emancipated at the close of the Civil War, they leveraged the other benefits of their prior status—political and social connections that gave them access to additional opportunities—and recovered their wealth fully within three generations.[5] Despite this concentration of wealth, much of the South remained impoverished for decades after the Civil War and continues to lag many Northern states.

More profound disparities emerged during the Industrial Revolution in the 1800s, which brought new tools and processes that enabled economies of scale in industry. Steam power also became available, transforming the transportation of goods so that mass production became a viable business model. At the same time, automation changed how jobs were performed, causing work to shift from farms to factories. New methods were applied to existing work, such as textiles, and new products, like machinery and equipment, were manufactured to fuel industrial growth. The scale would enable owners to accumulate greater wealth than ever before.

An influx of workers into cities led to early concentrations of poverty. Farm workers displaced by automation relocated to cities where employment opportunities were available, but these same cities also drew new immigrants seeking employment. The immigrants expanded the workforce and also became consumers, fueling economic growth. Nonetheless, employers had significant advantages, and workers often received low wages. As families struggled financially, children were drawn into the industrial workforce.

The significant scale of enterprises in the new industrial economy enabled wealth accumulation at multiples of

---

[5] Philipp Ager, Leah Boustan and Katherine Eriksson, The Intergenerational Effects of a Large Wealth Shock: White Southerners after the Civil War, American Economic Review 2021, 111(11): 3767–3794.

the wealth created in the simpler 18th-century economy. Industrialists in the second half of the 19th century overtook the wealth of earlier millionaires through their success in railroads, oil, and steel. Mark Twain labeled this period the Gilded Age to describe the concurrence of superficial prosperity and deep-seated social inequality. Some of the wealthiest Americans in early U.S. history are listed in the table below.

Name	Industry	Year	Wealth	2025 dollars
Stephen Girard	Banking	1831	$ 8 million	$292 million
John Jacob Astor	Fur trade, real estate	1848	25 million	1 billion
Cornelius Vanderbilt	Shipping, railroads	1877	105 million	3 billion
William Vanderbilt	Railroads	1920	100 million	2 billion
Edward S. Harkness (1940)	Oil	1918	125 million	2 billion
J. Ogden Armour (1927)	Packing	1918	125 million	2 billion
William Rockefeller (1922)	Oil, railroads	1918	150 million	3 billion
George F. Baker (1931)	Banking	1931	150 million	3 billion
Andrew Carnegie (1919)	Steel	1918	200 million	6 billion
Henry Clay Frick (1919)	Coke, steel	1918	225 million	7 billion
John D. Rockefeller (1937)	Oil	1937	1 billion	30 billion

Great wealth consolidated among a small number of major industrialists, called *robber barons* by the press at the time. By 1900, wealth disparity was well-entrenched and would take decades to narrow. There were between 4,000 and 5,000 millionaires, representing less than 1% of the population. The top 2% of households held one-third of the nation's wealth, and the top 10% controlled three-quarters. A growing middle class of business owners, managers, government workers, and professionals also emerged, representing about 30% of households. The bottom 60% to 70% of households, including a significant number of recent immigrants and Black Americans, comprised workers in factories, agriculture, mining, transportation, or services jobs.

This skewed business climate persisted into the first few decades of the 20th century, which were shaped by the introduction of the automobile, the establishment of transcontinental telephone service, the increasing electrification of American homes, and the emergence of consumer brands. Income disparity peaked in 1928 when the top 1% of households received 24% of all pretax income. Economic growth during the *Roaring Twenties* came to an end with the 1929 stock market crash. This marked the culmination of several decades of conspicuous consumption by the wealthy elite, known as the High Society, while many in the working class struggled to meet their basic needs.

The crash and the subsequent Great Depression devastated families in the working and middle classes, with significant losses among the wealthy. Those with wealth heavily invested in the stock market experienced some of the most significant losses. At the same time, those with liquidity could purchase distressed assets and benefit from the growth that would occur when the economy recovered. Unfortunately, the Herbert Hoover presidential administration, in power from 1929 to early 1933, was unable to end the depression, which deepened, and unemployment peaked at 25% by the end of his presidency.

Mid-Century Narrowing of the Income Gap

The Franklin D. Roosevelt administration began in 1933 with an ambitious plan to end the Great Depression and rebuild the economy. The stock market crash and subsequent Depression resulted from an unregulated free market. So, Roosevelt implemented key reforms over several years that restored the U.S. economy, resulting in decades of balanced growth and the lowest income disparity of the 20th century.

The day after he took office, Roosevelt called a national bank holiday. He worked with Congress to pass the Emergency Banking Act of 1933, which aimed to restore confidence in the banking system and prevent any further bank runs. It closed banks for a few days to establish a structure that ensured a stable banking system, and then the banks were reopened once examiners could certify that they met the liquidity and other requirements.

Three months later, the Glass-Steagall Act of 1933 was signed into law. This act required banks to separate their commercial and investment banking activities to limit the impact on customer deposits from speculative market investments. It also established the Federal Open Market Committee (FOMC) of the Federal Reserve and the Federal Deposit Insurance Corporation (FDIC) to safeguard depositors against bank failures.

Market reforms, including the Securities Act of 1933 and the Securities Exchange Act of 1934, established a regulatory framework over the stock market that previously lacked objective standards, exposing investors to the risks that emerged following the 1929 crash. These reforms were crucial in reestablishing investor confidence, enabling the market to thrive for decades. A significant share of U.S. wealth is still held in the stock market.

New Deal programs put millions of Americans back to work between 1933 and the start of World War II, which created many more jobs in support of the war effort. The Civil Works Administration employed millions in 1933 and 1934 to build infrastructure. This was continued by the Works Progress

Administration, which employed millions more between 1935 and 1943. The Civilian Conservation Corps, one of the most popular programs of its era, was designed to employ unmarried young men and focused on developing national and state natural resources.

During the Great Depression, many homeowners fell behind on payments not only for their mortgages but also for real estate taxes. The Home Owners Loan Corporation (HOLC), established in 1933, refinanced more than 1 million loans in just two years, saving up to 80% of those homeowners from foreclosure. While the HOLC ultimately foreclosed on about 20% of the refinanced loans that became delinquent for more than a year, they renovated homes and rented them out pending sale. They sold the foreclosed properties slowly to avoid affecting housing prices.

The Federal Housing Administration (FHA) was one of the most significant tools from the New Deal that contributed to the expansion of the middle class. FHA insurance enabled more families to qualify for mortgages and own a home, which drove a boom in housing development for several decades. For many families, their home is their most significant asset and has helped many families build wealth. As noted in the previous chapter, the economic benefits from this program were not shared with Black American families, who were excluded from participation not only in the program but from communities that were qualified to receive FHA coverage.

The middle class expanded in tandem with the broader economy. The working class benefited from several key labor reforms, including the National Labor Relations Act of 1935, which established the National Labor Relations Board, and the Fair Labor Standards Act of 1938 (FLSA), which introduced the federal minimum wage and established overtime requirements for work exceeding 40 hours per week.

The New Deal was a net positive for the national economy and helped many white families establish middle-class roots. However, its programs also discriminated against Black Americans in employment and housing, with implications that persist today. The exclusion of many jobs held by Black Americans from coverage under FLSA and the exclusion of Black Americans from suburban communities in which white families built significant middle-class wealth collectively undermined the ability of most Black Americans to gain financial independence for decades to follow.

During World War II, the economy was robust due to government spending and the middle class experienced significant growth. Income disparity was at its lowest between World War II and the 1970s, although Black Americans did not share in much of the middle-class expansion. Because of the discriminatory housing policy, Black Americans were not able to gain employment in some growth areas because they could not access nearby housing. The Fair Housing Act of 1968 put an end to *redlining*, but at that point, the homes that white families purchased in the 1940s and 1950s were not affordable for Black Americans seeking to buy into those communities.

The New Deal significantly reduced overall income inequality, and the World War II economy continued to show growth that was shared broadly across income levels, although not across ethnic groups. Income disparity in the U.S. remained at its lowest levels between 1950 and 1980, characterized by stable economic growth of 3% to 4%. The balance of regulation, worker protections, and a progressive income tax system, which will be explained in Chapter 5, supported these results.

Return of Wider Income Disparity

The income disparity in the U.S. began to grow again in the 1980s and has continued to widen since then. It is now at the same level as before the 1929 stock market crash. To illustrate the trend, the chart below compares mean and median incomes since 1980, showing how the gap between the mean and median has widened. Data published by the U.S. Census Bureau is used to ensure that the measures were based on a consistent data source. Before the start of the Reagan administration, the average income was only 18% higher than the median; by 2022, it had increased to 42% higher than the median. As the median drops away, a growing share of the population is losing ground, with the higher-income elite driving the average higher and thus widening the gap between low-income and upper-income households.

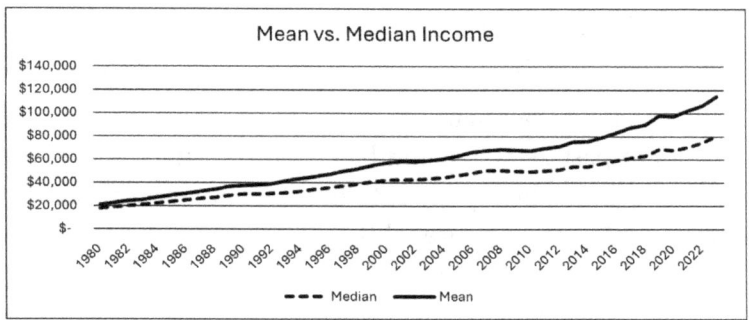

To better understand our current situation, I examined Internal Revenue Service data segmented by percentile groups for 2022, the latest available information at the time of publication. I summarized some key points in the table below. There were approximately 154 million households in the U.S. in 2022. Looking at the bottom rows of the table, income in most households falls within a narrow range; many Americans may not realize how astronomically high the upper incomes are. On average, each of the top 1,500 households earns over 10,000 times as much as each of the households in the bottom 50%, and the next 13,500 households each have 1,500 times the income of the bottom 50%. This indicates significant income disparity. The table on the left below shows the minimum income threshold for each income tier, and the table on the right below shows the average income within each income grouping.

Cumulative Tier	Households	Minimum Income
Top 0.001%	1,500	$85,465,000
Top 0.01%	15,000	17,855,000
Top 0.1%	153,000	3,272,000
Top 1%	1,538,000	663,000
Top 5%	7,690,000	262,000
Top 10%	15,380,000	179,000
Top 20%	30,760,000	117,000
Top 30%	46,140,000	86,000
Top 40%	61,521,000	65,000
Top 50%	76,901,000	50,000
Bottom 50%	76,901,000	0

Income Tier	Households	Average Income
Top 0.001%	1,500	$226,059,000
99.99%-99.999%	13,500	32,623,000
99.90%-99.99%	138,000	6,347,000
99.00%-99.90%	1,385,000	1,179,000
95.00%-98.99%	6,152,000	380,000
90.00%-94.99%	7,690,000	213,000
80.00%-89.99%	15,380,000	143,000
70.00%-79.99%	15,380,000	100,000
60.00%-69.99%	15,380,000	75,000
50.00%-59.99%	15,380,000	58,000
Up to 50%	76,901,000	22,000

The media has popularized discussion about the top 1% during the past 20 years, and based on the tables above, the top 1% is undoubtedly an elite group. The average income across all 1.5 million households in the top 1% is $2.1 million, but there is a broad range of incomes within the top 1%, reaching unimaginably high levels. Just 1,500 households, the top 0.001%, earned an average of over $200 million in

2022, with none reporting an income below $85 million. That group includes sports and entertainment figures, top business leaders, and successful investors.

Broadening the lens, research often examines the population for tax analysis in blocks of 20%, each known as a quintile. According to data from the U.S. Census Bureau, the share of income received by the top quintile of households has increased steadily over the past 50 years. From 1973 through 2023, the top 20% of households increased their share of income from 43.9% to 51.9%. The offset to this gain was distributed across every other quintile; the bottom 40% experienced the most significant loss. These statistics are more pronounced among the top 1%, comprising approximately 1.5 million households. Their share of total income doubled from about 10% in the 1970s to over 20% today, while the share for the bottom quintile of earners dropped from 4.1% to 3.1%.

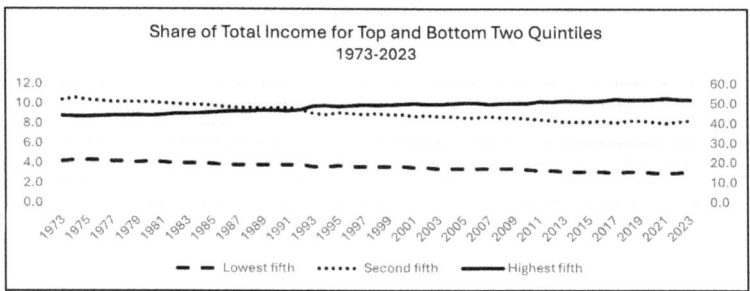

There was no income growth for the bottom quintile because, starting in the 1980s, wages for lower-income workers stagnated. Some jobs in the economy pay no more than the federal minimum wage, which was established by the FLSA. The 1980s was a period of high inflation, and the minimum wage was $3.35 per hour for the entire decade. Not surprisingly, workers lost buying power. Thirty states and the District of Columbia now have minimum wage rates that range from $8.75 to $17 per hour, higher than the $7.75 federal minimum wage. The movement to set higher state-level minimum wages emerged because the federal minimum wage was insufficient for areas with a high cost of living. Some large employers, such as Amazon, McDonald's, Starbucks, and Walmart, have increased their pay for entry-level workers substantially over the past decade or so, surpassing the federal minimum wage.

Since the 1980s, inflation has increased the costs factored into the income threshold known as the federal poverty level. As a result, while the minimum wage would have generated sufficient income from one worker to achieve 94% of the federal poverty level for a four-person household in 1980, by 1989, that coverage had dropped to 57%. Each increase in the minimum wage from 1990 to date has never raised the percentage of the federal poverty level for a family of four that it achieves above 68%. The minimum wage in 2024 was at its lowest level compared with the cost of living—it is estimated to generate an income of only 48% of the federal poverty level for a family of four.

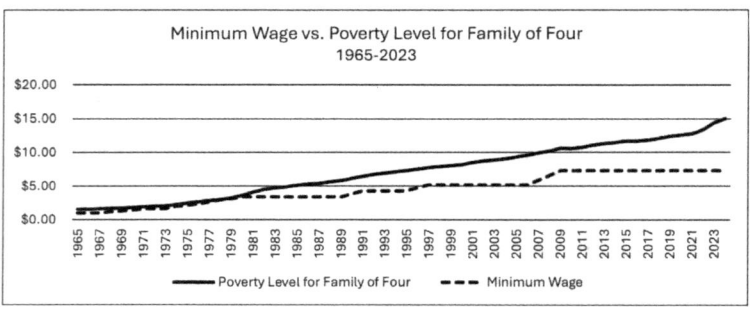

I am using the reference point for a family of four supported by one wage earner because having a non-working parent in the home significantly impacts child development, and the cost of childcare is out of reach for many lower-income families. It is also appropriate to model scenarios that allow lower-income families to make choices about raising children that many middle- and upper-income families have made.

Understanding Wealth Disparity

Given the level of income disparity we have observed, it is not difficult to imagine a corresponding wealth disparity. Lower-income households have fewer opportunities to build wealth than those with incomes closer to the median and above. We will discuss the persistence of poverty and the generational advantage of wealth in the next chapter—these two phenomena, taken together, help explain why the wealth gap is growing.

Furthermore, the impact of income tax policy on wealth accumulation is substantial and cannot be overstated. The rapid drop in the top marginal tax rate, from 70% to 50% in 1982 and then to 28% in 1988, was a windfall for high-income families, enabling them to increase their savings and investments. Not surprisingly, the wealth gap widened during and after the 1980s. Through a combination of tax policy, labor law, and economic factors, the nation's wealth growth since 1980 has primarily been retained by the wealthiest families, who have expanded their share of overall wealth at the expense of the working and middle classes.

Because very low-income people can save little to nothing and higher-income people can save a lot, wealth is more concentrated than income—the top 1% on income receives 22% of earnings, but the top 1% on wealth holds 30.8% of total wealth. The bottom 50% of the population, measured by income, receives 11% of earnings, but the bottom 50% of the population, measured by wealth, holds only 3.6% of total wealth.

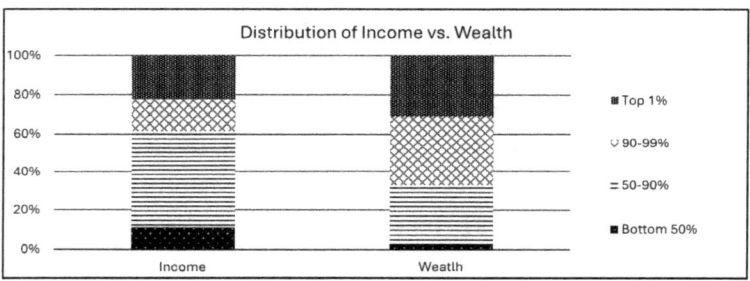

In 1963, the top 10% of households held 50.6% of the wealth, a share that increased to 61.6% by 2022. Because historical inequities prevented the accumulation of generational wealth for non-white families, the average wealth among white households in 1963 was two to three times that of all other households. Wealth in all households grew by 3.5 to 4 times between 1963 and 2022; however, due to continuing income disparities, white households still had an average wealth of two to three times that of all other households by 2022.

Also in 1963, approximately 90,000 millionaires and 10 billionaires resided in the U.S. These groups experienced significant expansion starting in the 1980s. By 1988, there were approximately 1.3 million millionaires and about 50 billionaires. Strong growth in the equity markets continued to significantly swell the numbers in these categories. By 2022, there were approximately 22.7 million millionaires, accounting for over 5% of the population, as well as 750 billionaires. While the impact of inflation may affect some of these statistics, the value of zero wealth for Americans living in poverty is still zero when adjusted for inflation, so the gap widens.

According to the most recent data from the Federal Reserve at the time of publication, total household net worth was $160.3 trillion at the end of 2024. The bottom 50% of households based on net worth held only $4 trillion, or 2.5% of the national total, while the top 1% held $49.5 trillion, or 30.9% of the total.

As people accumulate wealth, they can diversify their holdings to minimize the risk that declines in one asset class can undermine their overall financial health. Families in the bottom half of wealth distribution hold 86.8% of any wealth they have in their homes and retirement accounts. Among the top 0.1%, those two categories account for just 10.6% of their assets. Working- and middle-class families were hit hardest during the 2008-2009 financial crisis because residential real estate, where most of their wealth was held, lost tremendous value.

Distribution of Holdings by Wealth Tier[6]

Asset Category	Top 0.1%	99%-99.9%	90%-99%	50%-90%	All Others
Business equity	69.7%	59.2%	38.3%	16.0%	16.4%
Real estate, net	8.3%	15.3%	19.6%	31.8%	57.9%
Retirement plans	2.3%	8.5%	22.6%	30.9%	28.9%
Other assets, net	19.7%	17.0%	19.5%	21.3%	-3.2%
	100.0%	100.0%	100.0%	100.0%	100.0%

---

[6] Compiled from data reported at https://www.federalreserve.gov/releases/z1/dataviz/dfa/compare/chart/

The wealth distribution also reinforces the reality that most American wealth is built and carried in business interests. Financial business success often requires access to high-quality education and social networks that enable people to establish and grow their businesses, benefits that are rarely available to people living in poverty, which will be discussed in the next chapter.

4

Cycles of Poverty and Advantage

In almost every budget cycle in the U.S. Congress, effective programs that help address some of the barriers faced by people living in poverty are challenged and at risk. These programs, collectively referred to as transfers, include tax credits as well as benefits received in housing, health, and nutrition services. As earlier chapters have made clear, some segments of our population are descended from individuals who have had a prominent and longstanding disproportionate advantage, often ruthlessly exploiting others for their gain. The descendants of those with advantage are not responsible for their ancestors' actions, but they should understand and acknowledge the past and work to build a more equitable future.

After reviewing research showing that concentrated poverty and wealth tend to be self-perpetuating, this chapter closes with a look at income disparity after adjusting for: (1) income taxes paid by the wealthy on the resources they have available, and (2) transfers received by those living in poverty on the resources they have available. This analysis addresses the criticism that most data on income disparities discussed in public discourse is based on cash income rather than the resources ultimately available to the highest and lowest earning levels. Because these transfers are regularly at risk, it is vital to understand their limited impact on the underlying resource disparity while we work to address the root dynamic.

The Persistence of Poverty

Researchers and academics have been writing about the cycle of poverty since the 1960s. It was the foundation of President Lyndon Johnson's *War on Poverty*, which led to the creation of the Department of Housing and Urban Development, along with programs such as Head Start, Medicaid, Medicare, the Supplemental Nutrition Assistance Program (SNAP), and various training and employment programs. Several acts established federal support for primary, secondary, and post-secondary education. These programs help Americans whose low earnings place them in poverty to combat housing, food, and health insecurity, but without other interventions, they will not eliminate poverty.

The only way to eradicate poverty is to ensure everyone can earn a living wage. Short of that, efforts are focused on preparing children living in poverty to attain the education needed to climb out of poverty as adults. *Redlining* neighborhoods from the 1930s to the late 1960s created segregated communities that consigned many Black American children to communities with limited educational resources or opportunities for growth.

The U.S. Census Bureau studied educational attainment and found that approximately 9% of adults aged 25 and older had not completed high school. This group is overwhelmingly more likely to experience poverty in adulthood. An additional

28% completed high school but not college, with about half of them unable to enter the middle class.

Research shows that Hispanic Americans lag all other groups in securing at least a Bachelor's degree, followed closely by Black Americans. As a group, Hispanic Americans are more likely to be recent immigrants or the first in their families to be born in the U.S. Among Black Americans, many families have been in the U.S. for centuries. Still, as we have discussed, they were subjected to a century of systematic discrimination after emancipation from generations of slavery.

A ground-breaking longitudinal study evaluated the extent to which children in low-income and higher-income households have access to high-quality educational opportunities, measuring the impact on educational attainment and earnings in adulthood. The research began in the 1990s and followed 814 children across income groups for 26 years. In summarizing their findings, the researchers challenge the assumptions many Americans make about those living in poverty.

> *"Social science research has a history of highlighting the ways in which children from low-income families achieve at levels below their middle- and higher-income peers, often hypothesizing deficits, failures, and maladaptive practices within families as drivers of disparity. Our results suggest something broader and more systemic is occurring: Young children whose families have low income have dramatically fewer growth-promoting opportunities from early childhood through high school. These opportunity gaps largely account for differences in educational attainment and*

earnings of low-income children and their more affluent peers.[7]

These results reflect the impact of housing segregation and employment discrimination in the mid-20th century that consigned Black Americans and some others living in poverty to live and raise families in neighborhoods with a concentration of low-income families. These neighborhoods lack human and educational resources from which children can learn the skills to access higher-paying jobs and climb out of poverty.

Owning a primary residence has been a key wealth creator for middle-class families. Some families living in poverty who cannot overcome the barriers have also missed out on decades of property market appreciation and are priced out of the market. Homeownership rates have decreased as residential real estate prices have grown faster than inflation or the wages of working-class individuals.

A growing body of research shows that children from lower-income families living in mixed-income communities achieve better overall outcomes without limiting the outcomes for children in higher-income families. Indeed, children from higher-income families benefit from exposure to diversity that better prepares them for success in adulthood. Unifying diverse communities rather than perpetuating segregation should be an urgent public policy priority.

---

[7] Dearing, E., Bustamante, A. S., Zachrisson, H. D., & Vandell, D. L. (2024). Accumulation of Opportunities Predicts the Educational Attainment and Adulthood Earnings of Children Born Into Low- Versus Higher-Income Households. Educational Researcher, 53(9), 496-507.

Generational Advantage

While children living in poverty lack critical developmental and educational experiences, those born to wealth have many of them. However, this is not purely an issue of extremes since even middle-class families who may not have significant or any wealth live in environments that afford their children access to growth opportunities that can make a difference in building financial independence. At whatever level it exists, advantage begets advantage.

The phenomenon of generational advantage exists on a continuum. Advantages are cumulative, so as families prosper, their children get increasingly more opportunities to replicate and build on that prosperity.

The most poignant research on generational wealth accumulation was a longitudinal study that combined several complementary data sets. Researchers Fabian Pfeffer and Alexandra Killewald leveraged the Panel Study of Income Dynamics, which began in 1968, allowing for the study of multi-generational impacts as children of the earliest participants also became participants. The data encompasses all levels of wealth, but while it includes many multi-millionaires, it does not skew disproportionately toward the highest levels of wealth. They evaluated over 2,500 participants using data collected at three key points: the wealth of grandparents in 1968-1969, the wealth of parents in 1985-1989, and the wealth of children measured between 2013 and 2015. More than 80% of the children were aged between 25 and 44 when the measurements were taken.

The most important aspect of this research is that it evaluates the channels of wealth transmission, which extend beyond passing on financial assets through inheritance.

> "We find that more than half of the two-generational transmission of wealth is explained by educational attainment and channels that typically emerge in early adulthood, especially homeownership, but also marriage and business ownership. Our finding that educational attainment and homeownership are the most important channels for intergenerational wealth transmission is consistent with prior evidence documenting large and rising wealth gaps in educational attainment, the importance of family resources for the transition to homeownership, and the effect of homeownership on subsequent wealth.
>
> In contrast, gifts and bequests explain a small part of intergenerational wealth correlations. We considered that because grandparental death typically occurs during grandchildren's earlier adulthood, bequests and gifts directly received from grandparents may weigh heavier in offspring's ultimate wealth attainment. We find no such evidence. Instead, our findings suggest that investigations of the reproduction of wealth across generations should pay at least as much attention to early-life, indirect investments by parents and grandparents in offspring, including educational attainment and homeownership, as to direct, later-life transfers, such as bequests. Future research might explore the role of other, even earlier, types of investments

by parents, such as those to access advantageous neighborhoods, social capital, or cultural capital."[8]

Explicit wealth transfer is not the most significant advantage afforded to children born into wealth. The U.S. Census Bureau data demonstrates the significant impact of educational attainment on income in adulthood as well as the prevalence of home equity as an anchor of middle-class wealth. It is not a considerable leap to imagine family wealth plays a role in the ability to secure a graduate or post-graduate college degree or afford a home earlier in life.

While the research indeed supports the multi-generational benefits of wealth, it also showed that wealth persistence was diminished for Black Americans in the sample, which the researchers attributed to the impact of entrenched discrimination. There is also anecdotal evidence that as Black Americans gain wealth, they are more likely to share it with less-fortunate family members, so it is harder for them to accumulate. The elements of generational advantage and persistent poverty reflect an economy and society that do not offer equal opportunities to all.

Accounting for Taxes and Transfers

The official poverty measure (OPM), which is traditionally used to analyze the depth of poverty in the U.S., only

---

[8] Fabian T Pfeffer, Alexandra Killewald, Generations of Advantage. Multigenerational Correlations in Family Wealth, Social Forces, Volume 96, Issue 4, June 2018, Pages 1411–1442. https://doi.org/10.1093/sf/sox086

accounts for cash income. Due to their low cash-income level, individuals living in poverty may be eligible for specific public benefits contingent upon their family circumstances. These include housing support, health insurance, food assistance, and refundable tax credits. Higher-income taxpayers pay taxes on their various sources of income, whereas those in poverty often do not because their income is so low. Therefore, it is appropriate to evaluate them after considering taxes paid and benefits received to compare their circumstances accurately.

The major categories of transfers include:

The Supplemental Nutrition Assistance Program (SNAP), which helps families living in poverty to afford food. Formerly known as food stamps, this program is most often implemented through use of debit cards that limit recipients to certain categories of goods based on merchant codes. Many low-income senior citizens also qualify for and depend on SNAP benefits.

Medicaid provides insurance coverage for people living in poverty, including those with disabilities. The Medicaid expansion under the Affordable Care Act enabled over 20 million low-income adults to secure coverage they would not otherwise be able to afford. Over 10 million people with disabilities rely on support from Medicaid for care in their communities, where possible, or institutional settings, if a higher level of support is required. Almost one out of every four Americans receives benefits from Medicaid.

Temporary Assistance to Needy Families (TANF) only helps families with children or pregnant mothers who fall below an income level determined by each state or the District of

Columbia, usually set as a percentage of the federal poverty level. Program impact is limited because the federal funding levels have not been adjusted according to need. In the late 1990s, about two-thirds of families living in poverty received TANF benefits, and today, only 20% do. The federal allocation to the program is approximately $16 billion, and states provide an almost equal amount in local matching funds, benefiting around 3 million individuals.

There are several tax credits that are available to low-income families and individuals, some related to caring for children and others simply a boost to the resources for someone living in poverty. Tax credits are not means-tested—they are based solely on current tax-year income—so wealthy business owners who incur losses in a year qualify and receive these credits. The top three credits for low-income individuals and families are:

- The Earned Income Tax Credit, which is designed to provide support to low-income individuals and families, with significantly larger credits available to taxpayers with qualifying children. For 2024, the maximum credit was $632 without children, and ranged from $4,213 with one qualifying child to $7,930 with three or more qualifying children. It requires earned income, meaning the tax filer must have worked to be eligible for the credit.
- The Child Tax Credit of $2,000 per qualifying child, currently set to expire after 2025, is available to all tax filers with qualifying children but phases out at higher income levels: $200,000 for single filers and $400,000 for married filers. A portion of the credit is

refundable, so if the credit is greater than any tax due it can trigger a refund of up to $1,700 per child.

- The Child and Dependent Care credit of up to 35% of eligible expenses is designed to help families with children maintain employment. It has complex eligibility guidelines to prevent those for whom it was not intended from being able to claim the credit.

Even considering taxes and transfers, the data shows that the bottom quintile, bolstered by transfers, is growing more slowly than the middle three quintiles and the top quintile. If it had not been for tax increases during the Clinton and Obama administrations, the top quintile would have grown even more aggressively than it did, as the table below shows a spike after every tax cut during the Reagan and George W. Bush administrations.

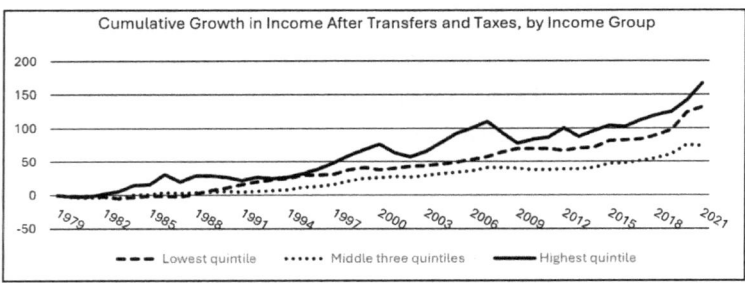

It is essential to understand that while transfers provide financial help and address housing, health, and food insecurity, they do not change the underlying income disparity. People living in poverty are unable to earn sustainable wages that would reduce or eliminate their dependence on transfers to survive. We should promote policies that address poverty wages before programs compensating for them are scaled back.

Cultural Barriers to Change

The percentage of families in the middle class has declined from approximately 60% in 1970 to around 50% today; however, it remains a significant and influential segment of the population. Among the middle-class today, many have worked hard to earn their place in the economy and do not always appreciate the advantages they may have had that allowed them to succeed, leveraging their talents, drive, and creativity. Without really understanding the history that led to our current imbalance, some in the middle class believe that (1) everyone has generally had equal opportunity, and (2) those living in poverty are not taking advantage of or capable of capitalizing on such opportunity.

Despite gains in distributing resources to people who are unable to earn enough to sustain themselves, we have made little progress in addressing the root cause of poverty. The factors that perpetuate poverty and skew wealth are complex and require solutions across society and the economy. Although some efforts have been made, they are sporadic and limited in scope.

- Housing: We must address the harm of *redlining* by investing in urban renewal that does not displace families but instead brings in other resources. Homeownership should be accessible to all who want it in mixed-income communities.
- Primary and secondary education: Resources should be equitably distributed to ensure all children have access to the same growth-promoting opportunities.

- Higher education: All students who wish to pursue college should be able to do so.
- Business formation: Because the majority of wealth is held in the value of businesses, there should be greater support for small businesses.

People struggle to share wealth because they are too easily convinced of their entitlement—and that others have not earned it. Some believe wealth is earned through hard work and merit alone, so everyone should have to do the work to share in the rewards. Others do not understand the barriers faced by those in poverty and are skeptical of them. More broadly, people take our current societal structure as immutable and thus only see opportunities for incremental improvements. We have had 250 years of mixed results in building an economy and society; therefore, we should still attempt, rather than shy away from, large initiatives to create a more just society.

5

The Federal Individual Income Tax

One of the most effective tools the wealthy have used to retain wealth is preferential treatment in the tax code. Today's income tax system dates to 1913, when the U.S. Constitution's 16th Amendment was ratified. Except for an earlier income tax enacted during the Civil War, excise taxes, customs duties, and tariffs were used to fund government activities from the start when colonists first arrived in North America and began organizing structures for governance. The current individual income tax system was initially designed to replace regressive taxes and tariffs based on consumption, which disproportionately affected people with lower incomes, with a tax that would generate resources from those with higher incomes. It then evolved over a century into a system that draws from a much broader cross-section of the population and has numerous provisions to limit the tax on those with middle- and higher-income levels.

Tax rates were substantially lowered in two cuts during the 1980s and have fluctuated since then as fiscal progressives and conservatives attempt to fine-tune the system to benefit different constituencies. This chapter describes the history leading up to the introduction of the current individual income tax system and its evolution over the past century, concluding with observations about the current rate structure and distribution of the tax burden. Our complex tax code and its history contain thousands of details, so I will primarily highlight rate changes and other provisions that best demonstrate how the tax code affected taxpayers at different income levels.

Two key concepts will be discussed in this chapter. When the percentage of an individual's income that is collected by a tax increases as their income rises, it is considered progressive, and if it decreases as income rises, it is considered regressive. Tariffs, duties, and excise taxes are considered regressive because lower-income taxpayers spend a greater share of their income on goods and services, making the taxes on those goods and services a larger portion of their income. The federal income tax, which applies higher rates to income that exceeds an increasing threshold as income rises, will average out to a higher percentage of income, making the tax progressive.

Government Revenue Before Our Current Income Tax

The colonies prospered in the 1600s and 1700s. The southern colonies exported tobacco, rice, indigo, cotton, and grains. The northern colonies had a robust fishing industry, exporting furs and pelts, lumber, and naval stores, including tar, pitch, and resin, which were used in the shipping industry. A robust shipbuilding economy also grew in the New England colonies. The European countries that established colonies benefited from having a source of valuable goods, which gave them economic power. In North America, Great Britain imposed limited direct taxation on the colonies as it sought to establish and develop them. Taxation in the colonies was primarily used to fund local government structures within the colonies.

Property taxes, poll taxes, and customs duties were the primary sources of funding for local governments. Property taxes were assessed primarily based on acreage, poll taxes were assessed on free men of a certain age, and excise taxes were assessed on other goods produced or consumed in the colonies. In addition to taxes, customs duties were levied on a range of imports, and in the southern colonies, the production and export of tobacco were also subject to taxation. The assembly in each colony would set tax rates and determine the allocation of government funds.

Following the Declaration of Independence in 1776, the U.S. was first organized through the Articles of Confederation. This structure was unsustainable because the national government lacked the power to levy and collect taxes or regulate commerce and was governed by a single assembly with no executive to lead the government. Another Constitutional Convention resulted in the new U.S. Constitution, which was ratified by the last needed states in 1789. I will focus the rest of the discussion in this chapter on the period from 1789 forward, following the signing of the current U.S. Constitution under which we govern ourselves.

The federal government was small at its founding, comprising only the Departments of the Treasury, State, and War, along with the offices of the Attorney General and Postmaster General. The cost was correspondingly small, so funding needs were limited. The U.S. began with debt from the Revolutionary War, accepted as national debt under Article

VI of the U.S Constitution. The debt increased when the government had to surge resources during the War of 1812 and the Mexican-American War. The government added only three departments in conjunction with westward expansion during the 1800s, resulting in limited pressure to generate new government revenue until the Civil War. Although Congress authorized up to $250 million in debt at the start of the Civil War, it proved challenging to find enough investors willing to lend, making an income tax necessary.

The Industrial Revolution began in the U.S. in the early 1800s, so by the time of the Civil War, there were already established and prosperous industries in the Northern states. As discussed in Chapter 3 on income and wealth disparities, a growing middle class and an elite group of industrialists were amassing wealth. The plantation economy in the Southern states was strong during the first half of the 19th century. When it became necessary to impose an income tax to fund the war, a tax base capable of paying was available, particularly among the states that remained in the Union.

The first attempt in 1861 to introduce an income tax, a flat 3% tax on income exceeding $800, lacked an enforcement mechanism and generated minimal revenue. Accordingly, the next session of Congress revisited the need for a tax and enacted a new tax through the Revenue Act of 1862. The act created the position of Commissioner of Internal Revenue, levied excise taxes on numerous goods, and established a progressive income tax system. The excise taxes were extensive and generated as much as 60% of federal revenue during the Civil War, compared to only 15% from income taxes. The lowest income tax bracket—3% on income between $600 and $10,000—exceeded what most Americans earned because the income tax was intended to target the wealthy. A second tax bracket assessed 5% on income over $10,000. A statement on the floor of the U.S. House of Representatives in April 1862 by Thaddeus Stevens, Chair of the House Ways and Means Committee, explained the underlying philosophy:

> *"In selecting the objects of taxation, the committee have found it necessary to visit many articles which they would have gladly spared. They have, however, laid no burdens on those who have but small means. They have exempted property and business below the value of $600, so that the poor man's tenement shall not be bothered by the tax gatherer. For the same reason, they have laid no poll tax. They have, no doubt, notwithstanding their best efforts, failed to equalize the burden to the extent to which they desired. They have attempted to raise the largest sums from articles of luxury, and from the large profits of wealthy men.*
>
> *"While the rich and the thrifty will be obliged to contribute largely from the abundance of their means, we have the consolation to know that no burdens have been imposed on the industrious laborer and mechanic, that the food of the poor is untaxed; and that no one will be affected by the provisions of this bill whose living depends solely on his manual labor."*

These rates were held for two years but did not generate sufficient revenue, so the Revenue Act of 1864 redefined the brackets and increased the rates—to 5% on income between $600 and $5,000, 7.5% on income between $5,000 and $10,000, and 10% on all income over $10,000. This act required taxpayers to file the details of income and property subject to tax and imposed penalties for failure to file and pay. The act levied licensing fees on every business generating over $1,000 in annual income—at varied rates for specific professions or businesses and a flat rate for all others—and enacted a stamp tax on matches and photographs.

In response to public opposition to the tax structure following the Civil War, Congress passed the Revenue Act of 1867, which restructured the income tax to a flat rate on income exceeding $1,000, still only impacting the wealthy. Though funding needs were reduced following the Civil War, paying down some debt was necessary. The Revenue Act of 1870 cut the flat rate from 5% to 2.5%, increased the minimum income to be taxed to $2,000, and set the tax to expire in 1873. Though this income tax has expired, excise taxes have continued to be a significant source of revenue for the federal government for many years.

By the 1890s, there was tremendous public pressure to reduce protective tariffs, which were blamed for industrial monopolies that concentrated wealth among an elite few while increasing the cost of goods for everyday citizens. Republicans lost control of both houses of Congress in the 1892 midterm elections because of the public disdain for tariffs. To lower tariffs, the government would need another source of revenue and an income tax to be paid by the wealthiest individuals was raised as a possibility. The Wilson-Gorman Tariff Act of 1894 assessed an income tax of 2% on income exceeding $4,000, a high threshold that would only impact the richest 1% of the population. In 1895, the U.S. Supreme Court decided in Pollock v. Farmers' Loan & Trust Company that this tax was unconstitutional because it was a direct tax under Article I, Section 8 of the Constitution and thus would need to be assessed on a proportional basis across the states. Efforts began in the early 1900s to secure an amendment that would enable an income tax.

Genesis of Our Current Tax Code (1913-1931)

By the beginning of the 20th century, the U.S. government depended on excise taxes, customs duties, and tariffs as its primary sources of revenue. All of these were regressive sources of revenue, disproportionately affecting lower-income Americans who spend more of their income on goods for daily living than those with much higher incomes. Following the 1895 Supreme Court decision overturning the last tax act, a movement started and gained momentum to secure a constitutional amendment to enable income taxes as an alternative that would distribute more of the burden to those better able to afford it.

In his third address to Congress in 1906, Theodore Roosevelt said, "The man of great wealth owes a peculiar obligation to the state because he derives special advantages from the mere existence of government."[9] President William Howard Taft was a champion for a constitutional amendment that would tax higher-income individuals, as happened during the Civil War. The 16th Amendment to the Constitution was initiated and passed by Congress as a resolution in 1909. It was ultimately ratified by 37 of the then-48 states and became law in 1913. The 16th Amendment states:

---

[9] http://www.presidency.ucsb.edu/ws/index.php?pid=29547

"The Congress shall have power to lay and collect taxes on incomes, from whatever source derived, without apportionment among the several States, and without regard to any census or enumeration."

Congress passed the Revenue Act of 1913, establishing the first individual income tax under the new power granted to it. The nation was at peace at the time, so rates were low, and the tax only applied to the wealthiest households—the rate structure included an exemption of $3,000 for single filers and $4,000 for joint filers, which was well above the income level of most Americans. There were approximately 20 million households in 1913, and only 350,000 returns were filed, so about 98% of households were exempt from filing. This isn't surprising, as approximately 60% of households lived on farms, and there were legions of working poor living in cities.

There were seven tax brackets with rates ranging from 1% to 7%, with the top rate applicable to incomes exceeding $500,000, equivalent to more than $15 million in 2024 dollars. That's much more progressive on an inflation-adjusted basis than our current rate structure, where the top threshold is well below $1 million. These initial rates remained unchanged for the first three years. The newly enacted income taxes initially generated less than 20% of federal revenue.

With war raging overseas, President Woodrow Wilson advocated for and signed the National Defense Act in 1916, which doubled the size of the regular Army. When Congress debated raising revenue to support the new costs, it considered the undue burden that low-income taxpayers would bear if consumption taxes were increased.

"No civilized nation collects so large a part of its revenues through consumption taxes as does the United States," complained Ways and Means members in their committee report, *"and it is conceded by all that such taxes bear most heavily upon those least able to pay them."*[10]

The Revenue Act of 1916 maintained the exemption amounts, so the number of people paying taxes didn't change. Instead, the Act increased rates across all brackets and doubled the number of brackets, including three new brackets above $500,000. The top rate kicked in at 15% for the portion of income over $2 million (approximately $58 million in 2024 dollars). Tax collections nearly tripled from $68 million to $173 million.

The debate also included a discussion of other taxes, as the estate tax was enacted at this time. In one of those discussions in Congress, Representative Clement C. Dickinson said, "Many of the enormous fortunes of this country far exceed any service the recipients of these swollen fortunes have ever rendered society, and the time is ripe and opportune to levy graduated income and inheritance taxes for needed revenues."[11]

The U.S. entered World War I in 1917, and additional revenue was needed to meet the significant costs. Congress passed a series of acts during and after the war that expanded the number of tax brackets from 15 to 21 and then to 56. Rates also increased substantially, with the top rate moving from 15% to 67%, then 77%, finally settling at 73%. Exemptions were reduced to $1,000 and $2,000, drawing another 3 million

---

[10] H. Rep. 64-922, supra note 3, at 3 (1916).
[11] Cong. Rec., supra note 4, at 10602 (1916).

households into the filing requirement in 1917 and growing to 7 million by 1921. After some progress had been made in reducing the debt accumulated during the war, rates were decreased gradually between 1921 and 1925 to a top rate of 25% on income over $100,000 across just 23 brackets. This structure held through 1931 when the Great Depression weakened tax collections, and rates needed to be raised again.

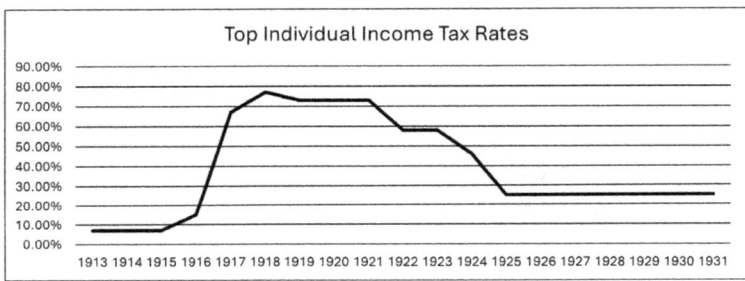

During this period, the new individual income tax system focused on taxing just those with the highest incomes using a graduated rate structure and an exemption of income below a certain level, eliminating the filing requirement for most households. Government leaders recognized at the time how significant the gulf was between working families and the middle and upper classes. About 25% of households were required to file a return during the war, but less than 15% were required to file before and after the war. Starting in 1918, income taxes provided approximately two-thirds of federal revenue.

Two accommodations to higher-income taxpayers related to capital gains were enacted in 1918: A separate 12.5% capital gains tax rate was enacted for assets held at least two years, and capital losses could be deducted against ordinary income. These provisions significantly benefited those wealthy enough to invest, given that the top rate on all other income was 77% on income above $1 million. Though gains at the time accounted for less than 2% of taxable income, it set the stage for differentiated treatment of capital gains from that point forward.

Expansion of the Tax Base (1932-1963)

Individual income tax collections dropped from $1 billion in 1929 to just $250 million in 1931. In response to the shortfall, Congress passed the Revenue Act of 1932, which substantially increased rates and introduced new brackets above $100,000. While rates for income up to $100,000 rose to as high as 55%, eight new brackets were added above $100,000 with 1-percentage-point increments, building up to a top rate of 63% on income exceeding $1 million. Though exemptions were reduced to the $1,000 and $2,500 levels, unemployment was as high as 25% during the depression, so this didn't significantly increase the number of returns filed. Increases in the national debt offset reduced collections during the Great Depression.

Individual income tax collections remained well below $1 billion yearly until 1937. Though revenue was needed, leaders were sensitive to the significant income gap and devastation of the Great Depression, so tax policy remained focused on those most able to pay. Collectively, the revenue acts in 1934, 1936, and 1938 substantially reduced the number of brackets while adding two at the upper end for incomes between $2 million and $5 million and over $5 million, with a top rate of 79% for income over $5 million. It is believed that only John D. Rockefeller, the richest man in the country at the time, paid the highest rate during the mid-1930s.

Michael D. Ward

In his June 1935 Message to Congress, President Franklin D. Roosevelt said the following:

"With the enactment of the Income Tax Law of 1913, the Federal Government began to apply effectively the widely accepted principle that taxes should be levied in proportion to ability to pay and in proportion to the benefits received. Income was wisely chosen as the measure of benefits and of the ability to pay. This was, and still is, a wholesome guide for national policy. It should be retained as the governing principle of Federal taxation. The use of other forms of taxes is often justifiable, particularly for temporary periods, but taxation according to income is the most effective instrument yet devised to obtain just contribution from those best able to bear it and to avoid placing onerous burdens upon the mass of our people."

The capital gains tax was restructured in 1934, eliminating the reduced rate but allowing for an exclusion of a portion of the gain that increased the longer the asset was held before sale. In 1938, a preferential rate was added back, and the exclusion was adjusted but otherwise retained.

Going into the 1940s, the U.S. government was building up defense assets in case it needed to enter World War II, which had raged in Europe since the fall of 1939. The U.S. entered World War II on December 8, 1941, following the Japanese attack on Pearl Harbor. Defense costs soared, and the need for additional revenue increased significantly. The revenue acts passed during the 1940s maintained and slightly increased rates but reduced the threshold for the top rate from $5 million to $200,000, which is still very progressive because fewer than 5,000 taxpayers, 0.01% of the total, were reporting income over

$200,000 in any year across the entire decade. The highest rate in 1944 and 1945, applicable to income over $200,000, reached 94% and settled at 91% thereafter.

The acts also lowered personal exemptions to levels that drew millions of additional taxpayers into the system. The number of returns filed increased from 20% of households to over 70%. With a large tax-paying base, the government introduced tax withholding from paychecks, the standard deduction, and per capita personal exemptions. In 1949, a separate rate structure was created for married taxpayers filing a joint return, favoring households with one wage earner and a stay-at-home partner. The income threshold for each tax rate change was doubled, effectively reducing the tax assessed on a married individual with a non-working spouse by half of what they would pay under the structure now only applicable to single filers.

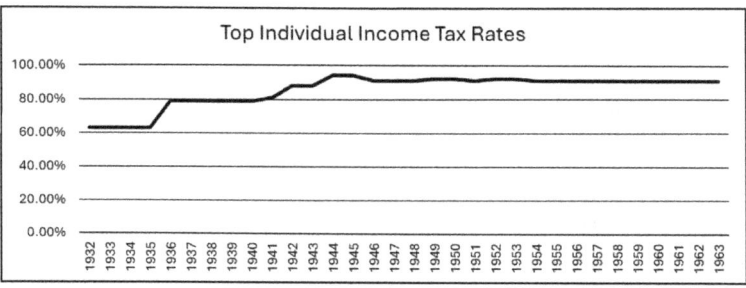

The brackets had never been indexed for inflation—the upper boundary of the lowest tax bracket remained at $4,000 from 1918 through 1940. It was then halved to $2,000 and remained at that level from 1941 through 1963. Because the brackets did not reflect the impact of inflation, more people at lower wages were paying taxes at increasing rates solely due to growth in their earnings. Throughout the first 50 years of the modern federal income tax system, public officials consistently held that income taxes should be significantly skewed toward the rich. The number of households with filing requirements started to grow substantially during this period, but this was also the period with the highest upper brackets in the history of the modern income tax system. Though more people were subject to tax, the rates were extremely progressive, and the highest earners had a very high marginal rate.

Rebalancing the Tax Burden (1964 to 1980)

By the 1960s, most of the working population had to file tax returns. Because taxes were withheld from paychecks, even workers who did not owe tax would file for a refund. The Tax Reform Act of 1964 reduced rates across all brackets and created several additional brackets at the lowest income levels, thus providing some relief to the lowest-earning taxpayers. The rates and brackets adopted in this act remained effective from 1965 through 1976. Though the rates remained unchanged, the Tax Reform Act of 1969 sought to ease the tax burden of lower-income taxpayers by increasing the standard deduction to $1,000. It also imposed an alternative minimum tax for the first time, limiting the usefulness of some tax preference items in avoiding tax. Congress articulated its approach in its Joint Committee Report, explaining the provisions of the act:

> *"The tax reduction in this act was carefully tailored to deal with what the Congress considered to be important national objectives:*
>
> *(1) Removal of all income tax from the poor and substantial reductions of the income tax for the near poor*

through an enlarged minimum standard deduction and increased exemption allowances.

(2) Obtaining substantial simplification of the tax structure for the great bulk of taxpayers by encouraging 11 million returns to shift from returns with itemized deductions to returns with larger standard deductions. This will increase from 58 percent to about 73 percent the portion of all returns using the simple standard deduction.

(3) Special tax reductions for single persons to insure that their tax burden in no event is more than 20 percent above that of married couples with comparable taxable income. At the present time (until 1971 when the new rates are effective), in some cases they are paying 42 percent more than married couples with the same taxable income."[12]

Tax legislation in the 1970s accomplished several objectives. The size of the standard deduction and personal exemption was increased, helping lower-income taxpayers, and the portion of certain dividends excluded from tax was increased. The alternative minimum tax and capital gains tax rates were increased. Toward the end of the decade, the Tax Reduction and Simplification Act of 1977 introduced indexing of the tax brackets and created a 0% bracket on the first $3,200 of income, with $3,200 added to each threshold above that, reducing taxes for those with incomes around each tier and excluding tax on the first $3,200 of taxable revenue. The most enduring tax change enacted in the 1970s was the introduction

---

[12] Joint Committee Report JCS-16-70: General Explanation of the Tax Reform Act of 1969

of the first refundable federal tax credit—the Earned Income Tax Credit for heads of households with children. This specific credit remains an element of tax law today, and its refundable nature has also been replicated for additional credits.

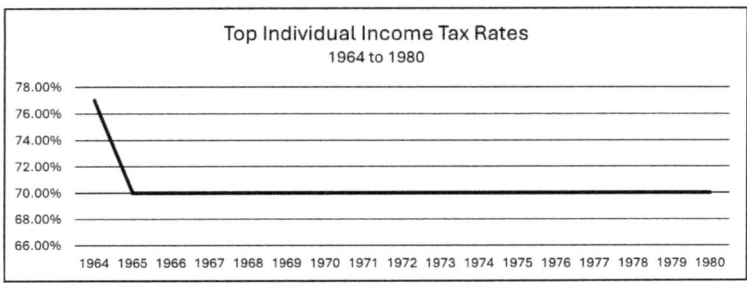

The Modern Era of Taxation (1981 to present)

The first seven decades of the current tax system showed that taxation is a dynamic component of our economy. It was used to raise resources during wartime, ensure that those with the most to gain paid a significant share of the government's cost that benefited them, and promote certain personal and business behaviors. Leading up to this point, it remained highly progressive, with top marginal rates of more than 90% for 20 years and between 70% and 90% for 26 years, with the minimum threshold for upper tax brackets as high as $5 million. Then came the 1980s.

The Economic Recovery Tax Act of 1981 (ERTA) significantly altered the tax structure by eliminating the top three brackets, dropping the threshold for the top bracket from $215,400 to $85,600, and the rate on the top bracket from 70% to 50%. This provided the highest-income taxpayers with significant savings above the $85,600 rate threshold, ranging from hundreds of thousands to millions of dollars at the highest income levels. The median household income in 1981 was $22,390. Households at that level experienced, at most, a 2% to 3% drop in tax.

Later in the Reagan administration, the Tax Reform Act of 1986 (TRA) introduced even more significant changes to the tax structure, reducing the top rate from 50% to 38.5% in 1987 and 28% in 1988, with only two tax brackets. By substantially lowering the threshold for the highest rate, Congress effectively eroded the progressivity of the tax tables, providing a substantial windfall to the country's highest-income taxpayers. Some offsetting changes to the lowest tax bracket and the values of standard deductions and exemptions may have had a mildly positive net impact on taxpayers at the low end of the income spectrum.

I had just entered the workforce when the TRA was implemented. I graduated from college with a bachelor's degree in 1986. From 1988 to 1992, the threshold for the top rate was so low that I paid a portion of my income tax on earnings at the highest rate. As a young staff member, I paid the same marginal tax rate as my accounting firm's managers, senior managers, and partners. The TRA also eliminated the deductibility of personal interest, except for mortgage interest, which disproportionately affected middle- to lower-income taxpayers who are more dependent on consumer debt. Those who could not afford a home were left with no benefit. It also curtailed deductions for retirement contributions.

The Reagan tax cuts affected federal revenue, so George H.W. Bush, who famously said during his campaign for the presidency, "read my lips... no new taxes," begrudgingly passed changes in the Omnibus Budget Reconciliation Act of 1990. This act capped itemized deductions at higher income levels, increased the alternative minimum tax rate from 21% to 24%, and introduced a new tax bracket with a rate of 31%. Higher-income taxpayers decried the increases, contributing to the election loss of George H.W. Bush, who was seeking a second term; however, it was still far below the rates from just 15 years earlier. The 1990 act also set a maximum capital gains tax rate of 28%, so higher-income taxpayers with substantial gains were not required to pay the new higher rate of 31% in the newly created bracket.

The 1990 changes did not meaningfully contribute to revenue, so the national debt rose by 60%. Bill Clinton ran for president on a platform of economic populism. The middle class felt left behind by Reagan's economic policies and was concerned about the growing national debt and persistent government budget deficits. Tax changes during the Clinton administration delivered on these promises.

The Omnibus Budget Reconciliation Act of 1993 added two new brackets at $140,000 at 36% and $250,000 at 39.6%, but because median family income was just over $30,000, the changes did not affect lower-income taxpayers. This was the first significant increase to the upper brackets since World War II, although these only restored a portion of the prior top rates of 70% during the mid-1960s through the 1970s or 50% in the early 1980s. From this point forward, the income thresholds for all brackets were indexed for inflation.

The Tax Relief Act of 1997 did not change the basic rate table but introduced several favorable provisions for lower-income taxpayers. The act introduced the Child Tax Credit, which started at $400 in 1998 for each child under 17, increased to $500 in 1999, and phased out at higher income levels. In addition to decreasing the capital gains rates, this act also excluded a gain on the sale of a personal residence of $500,000 for married couples who file jointly and $250,000 for all other filers, previously only available to taxpayers over 50 years old. It also introduced a student loan interest deduction of up to $2,500.

The pendulum swung in the other direction when the George W. Bush administration pursued tax cuts, undermining the revenue benefits of the Clinton tax changes. The Economic Growth and Tax Relief Reconciliation Act of 2001 introduced a new tax bracket with a 10% rate for taxable income ranging from $6,000 to $12,000, depending on filing status. The four top rates were reduced—dropping the 39.6% rate to 35%, the 36% rate to 33%, the 31% rate to 28%, and the 28% rate to 25%. These were to be phased in over four years and sunsetted after 2010. The Job Growth Tax Relief Reconciliation Act of 2003 accelerated the phase-in of the rate cuts in the 2001 act. It also significantly reduced taxes on capital gains and created a new category of qualified dividends, which are substantially all dividends from U.S. corporations taxed at the capital gains rate.

The Obama administration took office following the mortgage crisis that triggered the Great Recession of 2008-2009. Since many average Americans suffered financially, the Tax Relief, Unemployment Insurance Reauthorization, and Job Creation Act of 2010 extended the expiration of the Bush tax cuts and extended unemployment benefits for 13 months. It also patched the Alternative Minimum Tax, which had not been indexed for inflation and thus was increasingly hitting middle-income taxpayers who were not its intended target. The subsequent American Taxpayer Relief Act of 2012 made the temporary rate adjustments set in the 2001 act permanent but added a new top bracket once again at a 39.6% rate for income over $450,000 for married couples filing jointly or $400,000 for single filers. Certain deductions and credits were also phased out at these thresholds. The college tuition credit was extended, and the flagship Earned Income Tax Credit was expanded.

The first Trump administration enacted sweeping tax cuts in the Tax Cuts and Jobs Act of 2017. Some benefits accrued to the working and middle classes through a doubling of the standard deduction—though offset by the elimination of personal exemptions—and a family child tax credit. Most of the middle-class benefits, however, were set to expire after the 2025 tax year to reduce the calculated cost of the act and allow it to be put through as a budget reconciliation bill. Elements of the legislation that were negative for middle-class taxpayers were the $10,000 limitation on the deduction for state and local taxes, the elimination of the deductibility of up to $100,000 of home equity debt not used for improvements, limitations on the deductibility of casualty losses, and the elimination of miscellaneous itemized deductions.

The top long-term capital gains rate was reduced from 28% to 20%, and the rate for the lower bracket was lowered from 15% to 10%. A qualified business income deduction equal to 20% of income from self-employment was designed to mimic the impact of the corresponding corporate tax reduction so that businesses are not penalized for selecting one business form over another. It is thus favorable to the many small businesses organized as pass-through entities such as sole proprietorships, partnerships, or limited liability companies. While some of these changes clearly benefited middle-class taxpayers, they had a significantly greater impact on the highest-income taxpayers, for whom qualified dividends and capital gains account for nearly 50% of their total income.

While most Americans average about 80% of their earnings from salaries and wages, the highest-income Americans only receive about one-third of their earnings from salaries and wages and another third from partnerships, sole proprietorships, or S corporation earnings. The final third of high-income earnings comes from qualified dividends and capital gains taxed at the reduced rate of 20% rather than the top marginal rate of 37%.

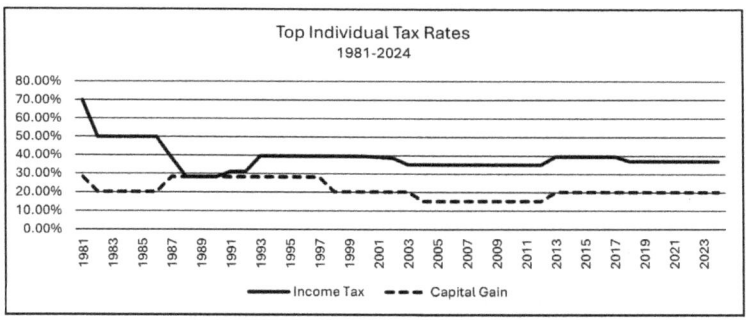

The Reagan administration changed how Americans and political leaders think about the tax structure. There are far fewer tax brackets, and rates are substantially lower. There seems to be no political will to consider structural changes, so all focus is on rates within the existing brackets and exclusions, deductions, credits, and other ways of impacting the portion of income that is ultimately taxed. Different views on spending and taxation have made tax increases more likely during Democratic administrations and tax decreases during Republican administrations.

Evaluation of the Progressivity of the Tax

There are many blogs and articles arguing that the tax code is no less progressive today than before. They rely on broad averages to support their claims; some use incorrect data. Throughout this chapter, I based my analysis and conclusions on data from the Internal Revenue Service. Here are three observations that support the conclusion that the tax is less progressive today than in the middle of the 20th century.

- The average rate paid by the top 1% was 31% in 1954 and 26% in 2022—clearly lower. If the U.S. collected 31% instead of just 26% of taxable income for the top 1% in 2022, it would have generated an additional $165 billion.

- Earnings for the top 1% are higher today than ever before. There were 560,000 filers in the top 1% in 1954 with an income of at least $20,000 (only about $240,000 in today's dollars) and 1.6 million filers in 2022 with a minimum income of $660,000, almost three times as much as in 1954 on an inflation-adjusted basis.

- Because of massive growth in higher incomes, the top 1% in 1954 had only 9% of the earnings and paid 24% of total tax but grew to 23% of the earnings and 40% of the tax in 2022. Their tax was 2.7 times their income share in 1954 but only 1.7 times in 2022.

The best way to evaluate the evolution of the tax system's progressivity is to see how far above or below average the income of the Top 1% is from the top bracket minimum threshold.

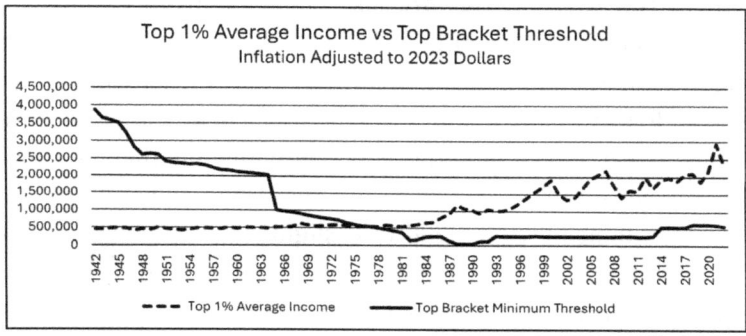

The declining line in the chart from 1942 through 1982 shows the impact of not indexing. Inflation affects earnings, so they grow relative to a fixed base. The first time an index was implemented was in 1984. Over several decades, the impact of inflation on Americans' income resulted in people of relatively modest incomes paying taxes in brackets initially aligned with the equivalent of multimillion-dollar earnings. At the same time, those with the highest incomes have an increasing share of their rapidly growing income taxed at the lower marginal rates in effect since the 1980s.

Other Tax Impacts

In addition to the federal income tax, payroll taxes significantly affect wage earners. They are decidedly regressive because there is a cap on earnings subject to the Social Security tax, which falls around the threshold for the top 10% of taxpayers.

Above that threshold, the impact of the payroll taxes trails off as: (1) salaries and wages exceed the cap, and (2) an increasing share of taxable income comes from interest, dividends, and capital gains that are not subject to Social Security tax. Because half of the payroll taxes are also collected from employers, small business owners and freelance workers who report their income on Schedule C, partners who report their income on Schedule E, and farmers who report their income on Schedule F calculate a self-employment tax when they file their returns. They pay both the employer and employee portions of the tax from their earnings, reduced slightly for the impact of a deduction for half of the self-employment tax. Adding the 6.2% employee portion of the tax to the bottom 90% of taxpayers with a diminishing amount hitting upper-income taxpayers, the average amount of federal income and payroll taxes paid at different incomes narrows significantly.

While the federal income tax tables are somewhat progressive, the different types of state taxes are generally not. At the state level, taxes on real and personal property are inherently regressive—those with the highest incomes spend much less on property taxes as a percentage of total income than the lower and middle classes. Sales taxes, like all taxes on consumption, also tend to be more regressive because lower- and middle-income households spend a greater percentage of their earnings on current consumption.

While these taxes are levied by states and localities rather than the federal government, and a handful of states have no income tax, they are not often part of the conversation about changes in federal tax law but perhaps should be. They impact the economic realities of workers across the spectrum and must be taken into account if we are to accurately measure their impact. Notably, if the federal income tax rate structure weren't as progressive as it is, households with the lowest incomes would disproportionately feel the overall tax burden.

Individual Income Tax Policy Recommendations

Before the 1980s, middle-income taxpayers paid tax rates in the middle of the tax table, and only a small percentage of taxpayers had income taxed at the highest rates. The tax table scale matched the population's earnings levels. Changes during the Reagan administration significantly reduced the number of tax brackets and the top rate from 70% to 28%. For six years, the threshold for the top rate was so low that recent college graduates were paying a portion of tax at the top rate. While some progressivity returned with the Clinton administration's changes, and there are now seven brackets, the top 1% are now paying a lower percentage, even though their incomes are at historic highs. It is not unreasonable for the wealthiest Americans to pay a higher rate as their incomes soar. Congress should add back brackets above the current top bracket with higher rates at those new top levels.

The state and local income tax cap of $10,000 is so low it hits middle-income taxpayers. Though it also disadvantages high-income taxpayers, eliminating it will reduce federal revenue by as much as $200 billion. Raising the cap to $20,000 is a compromise that would limit the impact on middle-income families while also limiting the impact on federal revenue.

Most provisions of President Donald Trump's Tax Cuts and Jobs Act of 2017 that were set to expire after 2025 have just been made permanent in legislation passed by Congress in July 2025. The state and local income tax cap of $10,000 through 2025 has been raised to $40,000 for tax years 2025 through 2029, subject to some income limitations. The higher level reduces the negative impact on middle-income taxpayers during those years; however, the cap reverts to $10,000 after 2029. Temporary deductions have been added for tax years 2025 through 2028—$6,000 for taxpayers over 65 with incomes below $75,000 as well as up to $25,000 of tip income and up to $12,500 of overtime pay, both subject to phaseout for incomes above $150,000 or $300,000 for single or married filers, respectively.

Key provisions of the current tax code that favor the highest incomes:

- Lower rates on capital gains and qualified dividends that reduce tax collections by approximately $300 billion. People with the highest incomes receive, on average, one-third of their income from gains that their wealth enables them to generate through investment.

- The mortgage interest deduction reduces tax collections by approximately $50 billion. Even with a limit on the maximum indebtedness that qualifies, taxpayers can deduct tens of thousands of dollars.

- Deducting the full appreciated value of donated assets without having to recognize the gain. Most taxpayers use already-taxed cash to make donations, but those with stocks that have appreciated in value can donate the stock itself rather than sell it and pay tax on the gain. While middle-class taxpayers can also benefit, there is no upper limit. A CEO with millions of dollars in appreciated stock can get a deduction for massive gifts without being taxed on the appreciation.

The value of taxes lost to deductions and exclusions should be individually quantified so they can be effectively compared with outlays for similar support for those with low incomes. Comparisons should be drawn between:

- Mortgage assistance in the form of a tax deduction, at approximately $50 billion versus the cost of housing assistance, which is roughly $60 billion.
- Healthcare assistance in the form of pretax deductions for employee health insurance worth approximately $300 billion versus Medicaid, which is approximately $600 billion.

Taxes fund the government structures that enable people to accumulate wealth, and the bulk of the nation's wealth is reflected in the market value of businesses. Businesses attract investment because markets are competitive and regulated. Companies grow and prosper because they have access to a skilled and educated workforce. Business risks are reduced because the government enforces laws against fraud and corruption, thereby promoting a more transparent and accountable environment. The activities that generate that wealth should be taxed appropriately to support these systems that make them possible.

6

Labor Practices

Forced labor was a persistent aspect of human civilization for thousands of years, and it is also part of the American story. It would be irresponsible to discuss labor policy without acknowledging that for the bulk of human history, many laborers did not enjoy freedom or self-determination. Before the Enlightenment, laborers—about 80% to 90% of the total population—were slaves, peasants, or serfs born into their respective social stations in life. There was no social mobility. They had limited if any, economic power and no political power. Social norms and religious expectations constrained individual liberty, which was broadly available only to the elite. Society was organized and governed by and for the wealthy.

Serfdom began a slow decline in Europe following the outbreak of the Bubonic Plague epidemic. Still, societies were largely agrarian, so there was never a significant concentration of labor in any one place. Religious institutions held substantial power and influence over society, often shaping individual rights and responsibilities within their respective religious doctrines. Belief in the divine right of kings, under which monarchs derived their power and authority from God, was prevalent from the medieval era until the Enlightenment. This doctrine established that subjects of a realm did not possess autonomy and were to be subservient to the monarch. This belief drove the extensive colonization undertaken by European monarchs from the 15th to the 18th century.

The colonists and conquerors used the religious foundation to rationalize their treatment of natives. They often brought missionaries with them on expeditions, attempted to convert natives, and then punished those who would not conform to their imported religious beliefs. They forced the Indigenous people to perform labor for their commercial purposes. When most of the Indigenous people were lost to disease or overwork, the colonists purchased enslaved Africans to perform the work.

Before the U.S. Civil War, enslaved Africans were the largest class of workers in North America. Labor practices on plantations were brutal and dehumanizing. White immigrants to the U.S. were free and able to earn a living, choose their employers, and change jobs at will. Before the Industrial Revolution, these workers were employed in smaller enterprises; some were indentured servants, and many were self-employed. While there was a worldwide reckoning with slavery through much of the 19th century, it is against that backdrop that we should understand the attitude of some industrialists toward labor.

The Industrial Revolution, which led to the emergence of large companies where economies of scale could generate substantial profits for owners, created the first large class of workers with freedom of movement to seek wage-earning jobs in different markets. However, these economies of scale in the numerous labor-intensive industries often disempowered workers.

Industrialization triggered migration from rural areas to cities, filling the urban workforce that new immigrants also supplemented. During the first several decades of the Industrial Revolution, there was no meaningful government oversight or regulation. Businesses were designed and organized to maximize profits, so work hours, work environments, and the composition of the workforce were not intended to benefit employees. Employers also took extreme advantage of children for hundreds of years until our better angels led to the passage of laws that protected children from dangerous jobs that robbed them of their childhood.

Organized Labor

Corporations and other large employers showed little concern for the plight of workers regarding the safety of working conditions, the adequacy of compensation, or the reasonableness of work schedules. They employed young children because they could pay them less than adults, who were already paid so little that families needed children to work to survive. Many factory workplaces were unsafe, and many thousands of workers, both children and adults, were injured or died in workplace accidents. In the U.S., the steel, coal, and railroad industries had high rates of injury and fatalities. Thousands of U.S. workers died in workplace accidents, more so than any other industrialized nation at the time. Unlike in Germany, Austria, Norway, or Finland, U.S. employers were not required to maintain worker's compensation coverage, so injuries and deaths were utterly financially devastating to working families.

It took a long time for the courts to acknowledge worker rights, in part because there were no laws in the U.S. that protected them. English common law, the fallback in U.S. courts, limited the rights of workers and prohibited collective action by workers as a criminal conspiracy. Hence, cases from the early 1800s led to the prosecution of workers who went on strike for better wages, resulting in financial penalties and, in some instances, jail time. Unions had some success advocating for wages, benefits, or safety, but employers resisted and attempted to thwart union efforts. Nonetheless, unions continued to form, particularly in the railroad industry, mining, and construction—fields that were highly hazardous to workers.

By the 1880s, unions were advocating for legislation to secure an eight-hour workday and prohibit child labor; thousands of labor strikes occurred in the late 19th century. Some unions were prosecuted under the Sherman Antitrust Act of 1894 following its passage, holding that strikes were an unfair restraint of trade.

Even after Congress passed the Clayton Act of 1914, explicitly exempting unions from antitrust prohibitions, prosecutions continued. Finally, Congress passed the Norris-LaGuardia Act in 1932, which prohibited employers from requiring a pledge not to join a union as a condition of employment, a practice that several individual states had outlawed in the late 19th century. In the absence of broad federal regulation, states began enacting worker protections in the early 1900s.

Federal Support for Labor

The National Industrial Recovery Act of 1933, which granted workers the right to organize into unions, was deemed unconstitutional by the Supreme Court in 1935. With the National Labor Relations Act of 1935 (NLRA), Congress re-established the right of workers to join unions, collectively bargain with employers, and take collective actions such as strikes. The act also enjoined companies from creating company unions. The preamble of the act stated it was required to correct the inequality of bargaining power. Most important, the National Labor Relations Board (NLRB) was established to:

- Guarantee democratic union elections,
- Arbitrate deadlocked labor-management disputes, and
- Penalize unfair labor practices by employers.

Some of the powers granted to unions under the NLRA were modified by the Labor-Management Relations Act of 1947, which focused on regulating unions, and the Labor-Management Reporting and Disclosure Act of 1959, which focused on protecting the rights of union members. With these amendments, individual states were allowed through right-to-work laws to prohibit mandatory union membership or dues.

The Social Security Act of 1935 established the first federal safety net for workers, though with implications far broader than just for the working class. In addition to the well-known retirement benefit, it also provides disability benefits. While it is a critical program implemented as part of the New Deal, it is regularly targeted, including today, for modification to limit its cost.

It is funded by a payroll tax assessed on both employees and employers. It is regressive by design, as all but the top 10% of earners pay the tax on 100% of their wages. A ceiling on the compensation subject to the tax exempts all wages over a level that only 10% of earners achieve. Because very high incomes far exceed the cap, the percentage of very high incomes subject to the tax is significantly lower than the percentage for working- and middle-class earners. The act also established the federal unemployment insurance program.

The Fair Labor Standards Act of 1938 (FLSA) expanded worker protections by prohibiting child labor in most industries, establishing a standard 40-hour workweek with payment of overtime above it, and setting a minimum wage. Personnel in professional and managerial roles are exempt from overtime requirements, although the exemptions do not apply for salaries below a certain threshold.

Business leaders opposed to regulation argue that if the government interfered less, employers could afford to pay more (but would they?). When minimum wages are increased, businesses adjust hours, staffing levels, and prices to compensate for the additional cost.

Minimum Wages

Between 1912 and the Great Depression, about a dozen states established minimum wages for women and children. However, the Supreme Court struck down a District of Columbia minimum wage law in 1923, which subsequently chilled further state action. During the Great Depression, market wages plummeted, and unemployment reached 25%. Many of those who could work still were unable to sustain themselves and remained in deep poverty. States again began establishing minimum wage laws, this time more broadly, covering not only women and children. In 1937, the Supreme Court overturned its earlier decision affirming the constitutionality of a minimum wage law.

The federal minimum wage was established by the FLSA. Initially set at 25 cents per hour, the federal minimum wage was adjusted every few years until 1974, at which point it was adjusted annually until 1981. Despite entering the decade with historically high inflation and unemployment levels, the minimum wage was held flat at $3.35 per hour for a full decade until 1990. It was increased six more times, the last to $7.25 in 2009. Fifteen years have passed with no further adjustment. This has had a profoundly devastating effect on low-wage workers, so 30 states and four U.S. territories have enacted minimum wage rates above $7.25 since 2009. State actions included legislation, ballot initiatives, and amendments to state constitutions. Currently, 34 states and the District of Columbia have minimum wage rates set above the federal level.

Critics of increasing the federal minimum wage argue that some small businesses lack the margins and pricing power to afford substantially higher wages, which may lead to their closure. This underscores the idea that the business model for some companies only succeeds if workers are not paid enough to support themselves. One reason there is persistent poverty in the U.S. is because the economy locks some workers into poverty wages. The system needs to be fixed.

Research by the Congressional Budget Office (CBO) has tied a low federal minimum wage to poverty and projects that increasing the rate will lift some families out of poverty, even after accounting for a potential loss of jobs due to the higher rate. In a 2019 study, CBO evaluated modest one-time increases to either $10 or $12 per hour or a more substantial increase to $15 per hour, which would then be indexed for inflation. The smaller one-time increases were, not surprisingly, expected to have a negligible impact because (1) fewer people earn less than $10 or $12 per hour before the increase, and (2) the small change would have a minimal impact on overall employment. The larger increase to $15 per hour, indexed for inflation, would impact 17 million people currently earning less than $15 per hour, as well as an additional 10 million people earning just above $15 per hour. CBO estimated that some jobs would be lost, though research has shown inconsistent results when evaluating the impact of minimum-wage changes. Significantly, millions would be lifted out of poverty.

Due to formidable market pressure and in the absence of federal action, major corporations have increased starting wages, and many now pay all workers well above the current federal minimum wage. Notably, companies have been able to manage their overall costs and adjust some pricing without undermining the business, as many critics of minimum-wage increases allege would happen with the increases.

There are three exceptions to the federal minimum wage that should be phased out. They are codified in a section of the FLSA titled Subminimum Wage:

- Section 14(a) permits employers to pay employees under the age of 20 for up to 90 days at a reduced wage, currently set at $4.25. For workers under 20 living in a middle-class home while they are starting to work, that may seem fine. For a young worker with a family to support, it is just another way to cut costs.

- Section 14(b) permits employers in retail, service establishments, or agriculture to pay full-time students a wage of no less than 85% of the minimum wage, limited to no more than six students and no more than 10% of hours worked by all employees. Students cannot be paid at a subminimum wage for more than 20 hours of work per week during school sessions or for more than 40 hours of work per week during non-school sessions.

- Section 14(c) permits certain employers to pay workers with disabilities a subminimum wage, provided they obtain a certificate from the U.S. Department of Labor's Wage and Hour Division. The wage is supposed to be tied to time studies to determine productivity against workers without disabilities.

The FLSA only applies to employees. In the current economy, many gig workers are classified as independent contractors or self-employed.

The labor policy of the U.S. government for decades has perpetuated an economy leveraged by keeping a portion of the workforce in poverty. People who can work full-time jobs should not have to live in poverty. If a business cannot succeed without paying poverty wages, then it is not a viable business. Thirty-four states and the District of Columbia have enacted higher minimum wage rates to which their economies have adjusted.

Labor Policy Recommendations

Human civilization worldwide has undergone significant evolution over the past few hundred years. The ruling elite no longer has nearly unlimited control over the masses. There is now a much larger middle class, and the human rights to autonomy and self-determination for the working class have been recognized. While the principles have evolved and many more people hold rights than before, the ruling elite still erect barriers to full participation in government and the economy.

Through the minimum wage, the U.S. established an appropriate mechanism to ensure broader equality of economic opportunity; however, the wage is not being adjusted to keep pace with the cost of living. A subset of the population, primarily business owners who employ a low-wage workforce, will benefit at the expense of others through potentially better profit margins with lower wage costs. The minimum wage should be adjusted to ensure that the lowest-paid workers can support themselves and their families.

Actions by politicians to undermine the NLRB's objectivity serve to diminish the effectiveness of organized labor in advocating for the working class and limit protection from workplace abuses related to worker rights to organize and collectively bargain. Developed countries with the narrowest income and wealth disparities most often have strong labor market participation and policies that protect worker health, safety, and quality of life. The U.S. economic system currently works to the advantage of owners, and laws should be enforced that protect the rights of workers.

1

The Origins and Taxation of Corporations

The corporate structure enables a business to raise and deploy capital from a diverse group of owners who may or may not be directly involved in its operations. For-profit corporations issue shares of stock to owners, which usually entitles them to guide the corporation's direction by electing members to a board of directors. Some matters may also come before the shareholders for a vote. While most nonprofit entities are organized as corporations, they do not issue stock and do not have owners or generate income for them. In this chapter, we will focus solely on for-profit corporations and their role in our current wealth disparity.

The purpose of highlighting the impact of corporations in this chapter is not to denigrate their value in a free-market economy. Indeed, by incentivizing focused capital investment, they have made significant contributions to the growth of the U.S. economy and have far-reaching effects on Americans' daily lives. The concentration of capital, though, has been to the most considerable advantage of those with capital to invest. It exacerbates the disparities when other segments of the population have been prevented from accumulating wealth by discriminatory laws and tax policies.

In colonial times, the corporate structure was primarily used by European nations to raise capital for building ships and launching expeditionary forces. Joint-stock companies, precursors to today's corporations, were chartered by European monarchs or representative assemblies during the Age of Exploration. These included trading companies such as England's Virginia Company of London, the Dutch West India Company, and the New Sweden Company, all of which focused on the Americas. Others, like the Dutch East India Company and the English East India Company, concentrated on India and Asia. The capital raised by these companies supported the development of new trade routes and, ultimately, colonization worldwide.

Colonial economies in North America were straightforward—their businesses were local and organized as sole proprietorships or partnerships. There was no banking system or single currency. Foreign coins, commercial paper, and barter were used to conduct commerce. Commodities were even used to pay colonial levies. Banks later proved critical in facilitating the flow of capital and interstate commerce, but their development was slow. Because financial capital is necessary to operate a bank, they would also be some of the earliest corporations in U.S. history.

Financial Institutions

In 1776, the U.S. had a primarily agrarian economy. There were two schools of thought among the founders. Thomas Jefferson, James Madison, and Benjamin Franklin, among others, believed freedom and equality were rooted in the land and hoped the nation would remain an agrarian society. Jefferson believed everyone (meaning white males at the time) should own land and be able to subsist on it. On the other hand, Alexander Hamilton led the group of founders who sought to establish an economy centered on banking, commerce, and industry.

The Articles of Confederation were adopted in 1781, creating a loose confederation of independent states with a limited central government. Some early leaders believed a national bank would be important in establishing the new country, so the Bank of North America was chartered as the first for-profit corporation in the U.S. by the Continental Congress in 1781. It was partly funded with deposits from the U.S. government, making the government its largest shareholder, and 99 private investors subscribed to shares in the bank. Thomas Jefferson liquidated the federal government's equity position in 1802, but the bank continued in commercial operation for decades and was absorbed into successor institutions through a series of mergers.

After the U.S. Constitution was ratified in 1789, the new Congress chartered the aptly named First Bank of the United States in 1791, raising $12 million in capital and becoming the new government's fiscal agent. Its charter expired after 20 years. A second national bank was chartered in 1816 with a

20-year charter that also expired. These were the only national banks before the Civil War, so from 1836 to 1863, only state-chartered banks operated without the benefit of a national paper currency.

By 1860, there were over 1,500 state-chartered banks. While individual banknotes were helpful locally, they proved challenging to use in interstate commerce. There were also several banking panics during this period. The U.S. government introduced paper currency in 1861, characterized as a demand note, to help cover the costs of the Civil War. This temporary war measure was made permanent in 1863 with the creation of the Office of the Comptroller of the Currency and the transition to national bank notes. Through an act in 1864, these notes were deemed legal tender for all debts, both public and private.

The Industrial Revolution

Rapid population growth in Europe during the 18th century spurred innovation, urbanization, and commercialization, which triggered the Industrial Revolution in Great Britain in the second half of the 18th century. One of the earliest industrial activities was the production of textiles, which spread to the U.S. in the early 1800s. The creation of factories enabled the mass production of goods on a large scale and at a low cost, which was a significant driver of economic growth. These early industries fueled growth in other sectors, including steel, timber, coal mining, and equipment manufacturing.

States began passing incorporation laws in the early 1800s, enabling corporations to form by adopting articles of incorporation rather than requiring legislative action. One of the first industries to adopt automation was textile production, with mills initially located in New England. These were primarily powered by waterwheels and built by entrepreneurs who replicated the mechanization of cotton processing they saw while working in British mills. They transformed cotton processing, shifting labor from home-based to centralized industrial operations. The Boston Manufacturing Company, often characterized as the first major industrial corporation, was established in 1813. It was followed in 1817 by Atkins & Pearce, which initially manufactured machinery used in textile mills and later produced their own textiles.

The Industrial Revolution significantly altered the composition of economic activity and employment in the U.S. Transportation networks played a crucial role in the development and growth of the economy, prompting the creation of corporations to build turnpikes, bridges, and canals early on. The steam engine was pivotal in accelerating the Industrial Revolution, allowing factories to be built away from water sources that powered mills. The steam engine was also used in shipping, starting in the early 1800s, and in railroads, beginning in the 1830s, which transformed the carriage of passengers and freight. This revolutionized commerce and expanded the reach of the young nation to the western half of North America. While early ventures may have been launched through partnerships, the ability to raise significant capital through the corporate structure drove rapid expansion and competition in these critical industries. In addition to domestic investors, Europeans were among those who financed the Industrial Revolution in the U.S.

Corporate power expanded significantly in the financial, transportation, and manufacturing industries in the 1850s and 1860s. Railroads had become a critical economic force, powering westward expansion with the movement of people and goods. In the 1870s, the oil industry transformed American life before electrification by producing kerosene for lamps. Many of these businesses started as partnerships and were later incorporated to access additional capital. Some aggressive and arguably ruthless business leaders began acquiring competitors and creating what would become effective monopolies in their respective industries. The significant wealth creation from these businesses led Mark Twain to refer to this period as the Gilded Age.

By the late 1800s, massive corporations ruled the U.S. economy. The structure and leverage of corporations enabled a handful of very bold and, at times, unscrupulous businessmen to gain immense wealth and power. Because corporations could not yet own stock in other corporations, industrialists created trusts that held ownership interests in various entities, and the trustees directed these empires. This structure is why the movement to constrain monopolies was called antitrust.

Article I, Section 8 of the U.S. Constitution grants Congress the power to regulate commerce with foreign nations and among the several states. The first law passed to regulate businesses, the Interstate Commerce Act of 1887, targeted the booming railroad industry. The Sherman Antitrust Act was passed in 1890 to outlaw monopolistic practices that inhibited competition. For more than a decade following its passage, the act had limited success in curbing monopolistic practices due to narrow judicial interpretations, and monopolies continued to grow.

A series of decisions in 1904 and 1911, however, successfully used the act to challenge and break up railroad, oil, and tobacco monopolies. John D. Rockefeller founded the Standard Oil Company in 1870 and, by 1900, had consolidated control over 90% of the U.S. oil market. The Supreme Court in 1911 required the monopoly to be dismantled, and Standard Oil was parceled out into 34 separate entities. Congress passed the Clayton Antitrust Act and the Federal Trade Commission Act in 1914, strengthening corporate regulation.

The Role of Corporations in our Economy

Corporations have been a significant factor in the U.S. economy for less than 150 years. Their number grew substantially in the late 1800s as the Industrial Revolution required the aggregation of capital to build factories and make other investments in durable equipment. They were leveraged to create immense wealth for a small elite group of Americans known as the *robber barons* by the dawn of the 20th century. Previously, sole proprietorships and partnerships were the most common business forms and continue to play a key role in today's U.S. economy.

Most founders were aligned around the ideal of a free market, comprising numerous small entities in healthy competition with one another, believing that competition would drive the best possible outcomes for society and the populace. However, the corporate form enabled businesses to scale to levels that stifled competition, thereby undermining the market's ability to function effectively.

The rise of corporations was a foundational driver of economic development in early U.S. history. The Industrial Revolution generated numerous capital-intensive business opportunities that corporations were uniquely structured to support. The U.S. led the world in the proliferation of corporations during the Industrial Revolution. States chartered over 20,000 corporations between 1790 and 1860. Industries such as banking, energy, steel, railroads, other transit, tobacco, and manufacturing all scaled considerably with the infusion of capital to invest in the growing economy's extraction, production, or delivery of goods and services.

At the beginning of the 20th century, the net income from incorporated businesses was nearly equal to the net income from unincorporated businesses. Their growth kept pace with each other for many decades. Most unincorporated businesses—such as sole proprietorships and partnerships—and some private corporations are closely held by owners who have an active role in the business. Publicly traded corporations, however, often have a large percentage of passive investors. For-profit corporations target earnings levels to ensure a return to owners who have invested capital, so they seek to control expenses, including labor costs, that will affect overall profitability. Therefore, for-profit corporations significantly influence the amount of value that reaches most workers' pockets and the amount of value retained by owners—contributing to, if not driving, the disparity in our society's wealth distribution.

Corporations generate returns for their investors in three ways—distributing profits in the form of dividends, retaining profits for reinvestment into the business to grow the value of the investor's holdings, or buying back stock from investors to reduce the number of shares outstanding and boost the per-share value of the remaining shares while returning capital to some investors. On average, less than 10% of corporate earnings are distributed as dividends. Most business wealth in the U.S. is in the market value of stockholdings or equity in other types of entity structures. The market value of stocks is often a multiple of annual earnings, allowing earnings growth to generate significant increases in market capitalization and, consequently, wealth for the holders of those stocks.

At the time of publication, the market capitalization of the largest publicly traded U.S. corporations is over $60 trillion.[13] Institutional investors, including pension funds, mutual funds, hedge funds, banks, insurance companies, and nonprofit organizations with substantial investments, collectively hold approximately 80% of the total stock value, thereby significantly influencing corporate governance. Although some billionaires hold as much as 10% to 20% of their companies' equity, independent individual stockholders generally have limited influence on the conduct of public companies. Privately held corporations have between $10 trillion and $15 trillion in invested capital. Individual investors much more significantly control them.

While acknowledging the positive impact corporations have had on the expansion of the U.S. economy, we discuss them here because, as the data shows, they also set the stage for much of the significant wealth disparity we see today, as owners

---

[13] https://companiesmarketcap.com/usa/largest-companies-in-the-usa-by-market-cap/

amassed great profits and wealth on the backs of lower-wage workers.

The Role of Corporations in Our Society

Corporations are created in law as structures through which to conduct business. However, the U.S. Constitution does not mention them, so laws have been passed to clarify their purpose, rights, and responsibilities. While some are created for a limited duration, the law allows them to exist perpetually, so owners and employees can change without disrupting a corporation's legal existence. This separate existence enables corporations to raise capital from investors who may invest due to the current leadership, but with the understanding that the corporation can generate value far into the future, even if key personnel or leadership changes.

Corporations are designed to exist separately from their owners, officers, and employees. While employees with management authority can be held accountable for specific actions, corporations ultimately bear financial liability and shield their owners from some legal and financial liability. Shareholders who are not involved in the operations are at risk of losing their capital investment; any abuses of the corporations they fund can only be addressed by the corporation's resources or the officers and directors responsible for ensuring the corporation operates within the law.

Once created and funded, corporations can hire personnel and acquire property needed to conduct the business for which they were formed. We expect their goods or services to be safe, delivered with quality, and supported for repair or replacement if they do not perform as advertised. We expect corporations to maintain and care for their properties and ensure that their activities do not negatively impact the surrounding properties. For personnel, we expect corporations to honor their commitments, treat employees with respect and dignity, provide a safe work environment, and compensate them fairly and adequately, so they can lead fulfilling lives.

Our laws grant corporations and their managers the right to set wages and hire and fire employees. The owners and management hold all the economic power except where labor unions are present. Most rank-and-file employees are ultimately protected only by the labor laws we have enacted and labor market forces that constrain corporate behavior. Over the years, these labor market forces have become less effective in protecting the most vulnerable members of our society, the working class.

For example, by 1960, about 45% of the private-sector workforce was covered under defined benefit pension plans. Since the 1970s, corporations have broadly stepped away from funding pension plans, and only about 15% of private-sector employees are covered by them today. The standard for retirement shifted from defined benefit plans, which admittedly are difficult for corporations to plan for and fund, to defined contribution plans that ultimately depend on employee savings choices.

Middle-class families in the middle of the 20th century often sustained their lifestyles by having one working parent, most often the father, however, as there were limited workplace accommodations for mothers to sustain employment and build careers.

Entities such as the Federal Trade Commission and the Securities and Exchange Commission, among others, ensure that all market participants play by the same rules and are not unduly advantaged relative to their competitors. Social programs enable low-wage workers to survive and be available to work, and corporate profits benefit directly from many elements of the federal government.

In the mid-20th century, limited international competition allowed U.S. corporations to flourish. At the time, counterbalancing powers to keep corporate excesses in check, as hypothesized by economist John Kenneth Galbraith, were in place—big labor unions, big government, and big consumers. Indeed, American corporate culture was centered on generating value across various stakeholder groups, including shareholders, employees, consumers, and society.

The period from 1965 to 1982 is sometimes referred to as the Great Inflation. During this period, oil crises significantly buffeted the daily lives of most Americans, driving up production and transportation costs for many businesses. There were several periods of recession, stocks were in a bear market, companies struggled with foreign competition, and job losses led to a rise in unemployment. It was a difficult period for corporations and society as a whole.

Stagflation, a combination of high inflation and high unemployment, hit the U.S. economy from the mid-1970s to the early 1980s. Monetary policy led by Paul Volcker in the 1980s eventually tamed inflation, but unemployment remained persistent. In the 1980s, corporate culture underwent a significant shift, prioritizing the pursuit of shareholder value over all other considerations. Shareholder value is maximized when costs are low, and labor is a substantial cost for many companies. The era of corporations having a larger purpose essentially came to an end, and the economy was centered on generating value for owners—people who already possessed wealth—while the working class struggled with low wages.

While the working class suffered, young urban professionals, known as yuppies, paid little attention to social responsibility and instead embraced materialism and wealth accumulation. The decade of the 1980s was marked by rampant materialism and greed.

Remarkably, the Business Roundtable, a group of corporate executives formed in 1972, issued a statement in 1981 that asserted corporations should be a positive force in society and highlighted their responsibility to customers, employees, and the communities they serve. This statement proved to be more of an acknowledgment of the prevailing beliefs than a commitment to the future. As a group, they edged away from this statement over time. They fully embraced shareholder primacy in the 1990s and then, in 2019, inspired no doubt by public disdain for corporate behavior, returned to the message that a corporation's purpose is to bring value to society and its stakeholders beyond the shareholders.

Corporations have a profound impact on our society. They also could not exist without the support of the federal government. Following the 1929 market crash, which resulted in severe economic losses, the government established the Securities and Exchange Commission to restore investor confidence in the functioning of the markets. As a result, the market has attracted unparalleled investment, both domestically and worldwide. The Federal Trade Commission ensures that the marketplace maintains a healthy competitive environment. Although corporations resist regulation, many enacted rules have protected consumers, employees, and the public, allowing the U.S. corporate environment to prosper with little fear of significant risk.

Although there are complaints that corporations are overregulated, the government performs functions that directly benefit them, enabling them to raise capital with the confidence of the investing public, engage in business, and thrive. For example, a strong military protects the economic interests of corporations and their owners by ensuring U.S. markets are safe from the ravages of war and maintaining a safe environment for domestic and foreign investors to put their capital at risk.

Because corporations are not mentioned in the U.S. Constitution, courts stepped in to grant them certain constitutional rights. The U.S. Supreme Court affirmed some constitutional rights to corporations in the following cases:

- In 1815, the Supreme Court held in Terrett v. Taylor that the Commonwealth of Virginia could not confiscate land owned by the Episcopal Church. This established a corporation's right to hold property without government interference, which is guaranteed to people in the 5th Amendment.
- In 1819, the Supreme Court held in Trustees of Dartmouth College v. Woodward that the State of New Hampshire could not alter Dartmouth's charter to make it a public university based on the contract rights affirmed by Article I, Section 10, Clause 1 of the U.S. Constitution.

- In 1886, the Supreme Court held in Santa Clara County v. Southern Pacific Railroad that the 14th Amendment of the U.S. Constitution confers on corporations a right to equal protection, effectively establishing corporate personhood.
- In 2010, the Supreme Court held in Citizens United v. Federal Election Commission that the free speech rights granted by the 1st Amendment to the U.S. Constitution applied to corporations and Congress couldn't limit their political speech.
- In 2014, the Supreme Court held in Burwell v. Hobby Lobby that corporations had a right to religious freedom under the Religious Freedom Restoration Act of 1993 and thus could not be compelled to offer contraception in its health plan, which Hobby Lobby declared would violate its religious beliefs.

We cherish the rights for individuals guaranteed by the Constitution. The extension of property and contract rights, as well as equal protection, to corporations is necessary for businesses to have confidence in spending or investment decisions. Since corporations are not sentient, only those who control them can exercise the right to speech or religious freedom. If corporations are an extension of the people who control them, then they should be taxed the same as a sole proprietorship or partnership whose owners have those rights as individuals.

While some segments of society today argue that businesses are subject to crippling regulation, the history of corporations reveals that unfettered capitalism is not an ideal to which we should aspire. Unfettered capitalism was also the genesis of tremendous abuses that required decades of legal action to constrain the worst impulses of capitalists.

Corporate Taxation

This chapter began with a history of corporations and their pervasive roles in our economy and society. As they wield significant power and influence, therefore, corporations should pay their fair share of taxes to support the costs of the system that enables and protects them.

The bases for corporate and individual income tax are significantly different in terms of the amount retained after-tax payment. Corporations deduct almost all expenses in arriving at corporate taxable income, so the only significant choice left is whether to reinvest or distribute the profits after the payment of any tax. Individuals, on the other hand, essentially pay tax on their gross income (from salaries or other sources) plus the net income from self-employment with only some deductions allowed. That means individuals still have to pay for living expenses, including interest on debt other than mortgages, beyond their tax bill. Accordingly, not all taxable income is the same.

While public policy debates often focus on individual or corporate income taxes as though each stands alone, it is illuminating to examine them together. Since 1960, corporate income has fluctuated between 10% and 15% of national income, while corporate income taxes have dropped from 33% to 14% of total income tax collections. Since individuals still have to pay living expenses out of their post-tax income, it does not make sense that corporate taxes should be the same percentage of total taxes paid as corporation income is of the national income.

The U.S. Bureau of Economic Analysis tracks the National Income and Product Accounts, which categorize national income into employee compensation, unincorporated business profits, net rental income earned by individuals, net interest paid, and several other categories. Americans receive, in aggregate, over $14 trillion annually as compensation for employment. Corporate profits, which are net of employee compensation, have been growing as a percentage of national income while shrinking as a percentage of total tax collected.

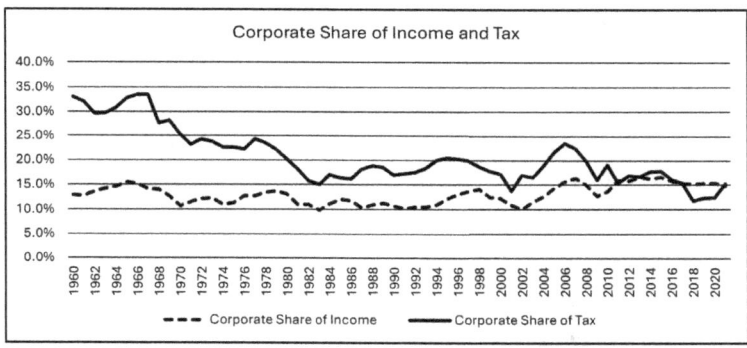

Before 1913, corporations paid only excise taxes, stamp taxes, and customs duties on certain goods they produced or imported. In 1909, before the ratification of the 16th Amendment, Congress used the excise tax form to begin collecting a greater amount from corporations. Net income over $10,000 was subject to a 1% tax. Following the passage of the 16th Amendment, the corporate income tax evolved along similar lines as the individual income tax.

Business earnings are taxed in different ways. Partners and sole proprietors pay tax on their share of business earnings at their regular income tax rates, but corporate profits currently are taxed at much lower tax rates. Then, only the portion of earnings distributed as dividends is further taxed, at either the recipient's regular rates or at the capital gains tax rate if paid by a domestic corporation and the recipient has held the stock for at least 120 days.

Before the rise of corporations, most business was conducted as sole proprietorships or through partnerships. Owners of businesses organized as sole proprietorships and partnerships, representing about half of private-sector activity and employment, are taxed on their share of business earnings as part of their regular income at prevailing individual tax rates. Tax policy should not favor one business structure over another.

Another way corporations exacerbate the wealth imbalance is by becoming a store of value for wealthy individuals through stock ownership. Years of profitable operation drive appreciation in the value of their ownership interest, and affluent investors, under our tax laws, can accumulate tremendous wealth without paying tax on it until the ownership position is sold. Another way the tax system advantages wealth is by allowing heirs to take a stepped-up basis to market value at the time of death, exempting significant gains that would otherwise be taxed.

In the Revenue Act of 1958, Congress introduced a provision in the tax code that allows small, closely held corporations with 100 or fewer individual shareholders to file a Subchapter S election, thereby being taxed similarly to partnerships.

Because taxes on S corporation earnings are taxed to the individual owners, I will group them with sole proprietorships and partnerships in this discussion to focus on separately taxable corporations, known as C corporations. Private-sector employment is split between C corporations and everything else.

Corporate revenue is generated by economic activity. A portion of the revenue is used to pay workers and purchase other goods and services. Focusing just on labor, if corporations pay more to their workers and are unable to pass that cost along to consumers, then income would shift from the corporate entity to individuals.

While corporate dividends are received by the middle class and well as the wealthiest among us, special tax rates are a windfall for the rich. Dividends were not taxed at all until 1936, when they were required to be reported and taxed at the same rate as regular income. They were exempted once again in 1939 and remained exempt until 1954. Starting in 1954, they were reported and taxed at the same rate as regular income until 2003, with the first $50-$200 exempt from tax between 1954 and 1984. In 2003, the tax rate for dividends was pegged at 15%, less than half of the top rate. Starting in 2013, the dividend tax rates were restructured and tied to adjusted gross income at 0%, 15%, or 20%.

The federal corporate income tax evolved alongside but on a slightly different path from the individual income tax. While corporate income tax rates rose during periods of war and substantial economic challenges, Congress also introduced a tax on undistributed profits from 1920 to 1930 to ensure that corporations distributed their profits to investors, who would then spend the money and pay taxes on the dividends. When the undistributed profits tax ended in 1940, there was no pressure to distribute cash, so corporations began building up cash balances.

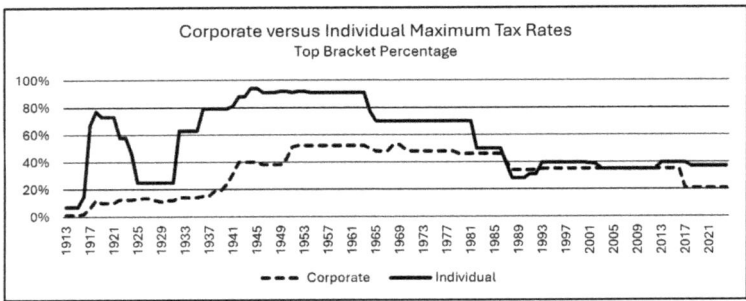

In the Tax Cuts and Jobs Act, from the first Trump administration, the corporate income tax rate was lowered to a flat 21%, and the law introduced a Qualified Business Income deduction equal to 20% of qualified business income as an accommodation to pass-through businesses. The QBI deduction, which was set to expire in 2025 but has been made permanent in recent legislation, does not fully equalize the result of applying both corporate and individual rates to the same income. The structure still disadvantages small businesses organized as sole proprietorships or partnerships to some degree. Corporations against which pass-through businesses must compete have a financial advantage over them, which accrues to the benefit of the corporation owners who have more after-tax net income as a return on investment, driving corporate earnings.

More advantageous tax rates for corporations will drive businesses established as sole proprietorships and partnerships toward the corporate legal structure. Corporations have more compliance requirements, thus raising the barrier to entry for a new business and inhibiting competion. Reducing competition that otherwise benefits consumers, workers and small business owners should not be an outcome of tax policy.

For a brief historical overview, the corporate income tax was initially set at a flat rate from 1913 to 1917, increasing from 1% to 6% of net income during that period. The first $2,000 of corporate net income was exempt from taxation from 1918 to 1927, and the first $3,000 of corporate net income was exempt from taxation from 1928 to 1931. All other income was taxed at a rate that increased from 12% to 14% over that period. The tax returned to a flat rate from 1932 to 1935, and then from 1936 forward, additional brackets were added. Maximum effective rates jumped to over 20% starting in 1940, over 30% in 1942, and over 40% during World War II from 1942 to 1945. There was a graduated tax structure until 2018, with a maximum rate in the top bracket ranging from 38% to 53%. A flat corporate tax was enacted, effective as of 2018, and remains in place today.

The 1917 Act also imposed an excess profit tax on corporations to tax the exceptional war profits that many companies were experiencing. It also encouraged companies to distribute their earnings rather than allowing them to accumulate in corporate accounts. Dividends would then be taxed. The tax was unpopular and was phased out by the early 1920s. It was reinstated during World War II and the Korean War.

The move to continually reduce the corporate income tax rate diverts critical resources away from the government, particularly when corporate income is an increasing share of national income. Yet corporate tax collections are declining as a percentage of total collections. If corporations paid their low-wage employees better, the U.S. might not need as many social programs. However, as long as working-class wages remain low, corporations should pay more in taxes.

Corporate Policy Recommendations

Corporations are a purely human construct, and their operations vary depending on the laws in the states and/or countries in which they conduct business. While we created them to enable the aggregation of capital to conduct commercial activities, to the extent they allow owners to wield outsized power relative to employees, society at large, or the environment, we can and should constrain them. Without regulation, they would seek to maximize profits by exposing workers to hazardous conditions for the lowest possible pay, polluting the environment if it is cheaper to do so, and acquiring competitors to dominate marketplaces to the detriment of consumers.

I included the history and role of corporations in society and the economy in the same section as I discussed the taxation of corporations for two crucial reasons.

> 1) Corporations, which enable Americans who already possess wealth to invest and earn a return on that wealth without exposing any other personal assets, benefit from the structure and protections provided by the federal government and should contribute to its cost.

2) Though some of the rights corporations have been accorded under the Constitution—holding property without interference, contracting, and equal protection—are necessary for them to function in society without irreconcilable conflicts, both the right to religious expression and freedom of speech cannot be exercised by an inanimate entity and thus are instead an amplification of the rights of the individuals who control and can shape a corporation's expression.

For these reasons, corporations should pay at least as much tax as individuals, and the dividends owners receive should also be taxed. The U.S. Supreme Court should also reevaluate whether the rights to free speech and religious expression disproportionately benefit owners at the expense of all others.

According to the nonprofit organization Public Citizen, thousands of lobbyists earn hundreds of millions of dollars annually to secure favorable tax treatment for corporations.[14] They have earned their fees with some of the most advantageous tax policies in American history. Corporations do not have to provide for a family or put food on the table like everyday Americans; tax savings for corporations benefit the wealthy who own them.

---

[14] https://www.citizen.org/news/corporations-are-spending-millions-on-lobbying-to-avoid-taxes/ and https://www.citizen.org/article/corporate-america-dominates-tax-lobbying/

Shared Self-Governance

The U.S. was founded on the belief that people of goodwill from diverse backgrounds can build a nation together through a structure of shared self-governance. Most of the progress the U.S. has made "to form a more perfect union" as set out in the U.S. Constitution has been the result of government action. The constitutional structure played a critical role in efforts to end slavery, regulate corporate behavior, and address economic imbalances resulting from industrialization. Just as America has struggled with sharing wealth, however, it has also struggled with sharing power.

As described in earlier chapters, wealth and power are often closely correlated because those with wealth usually leverage it to retain or gain power or influence those who already hold power. The individual income tax code, initially designed to limit the burden on the working class, has been modified over time to limit instead the burden on those with the most significant incomes and wealth.

Some movements began in the community but required government action to endure. For instance, colonists felt oppressed by a distant parliament and monarchy, so they gathered as independent jurisdictions and then decided to declare independence from Great Britain and form a government. Abolitionists pressed their case against slavery for years. They ultimately elected a president and Congress that acted to enforce constitutional ideals and implemented laws to change the course of the country.

Following the Civil War, the powers of state governments were leveraged by factions seeking to thwart progress, and they achieved their discriminatory and heart-wrenching goals with devastating success. The federal courts, largely vestiges of prior culture and regimes, supported the state action at the time. True reform required amendments to the U.S. Constitution, which were accomplished through legislative action, first at the federal level and then ratified at the state level. Additional laws were needed to provide structure to the reforms, which were often initially stated in brief and concise terms. Programs to counterbalance the impact of a free market—the tax and labor policies discussed in earlier chapters—required legislative action to be put in place.

Democratic participation is thus essential to ensure a robust debate, allowing all views to be incorporated into the policy-making process. The people of the U.S. charted and navigated the course of our nation through their commitment to shared self-governance. This chapter reviews its history, tracing how civilization has evolved from the earliest recorded democracies to our democratic republic of today. It took almost 200 years for the U.S. to guarantee broad suffrage, yet voter suppression activities are still visible in many states. The right to vote has power, and some special interests want to limit that power.

The History of Democracy

The term civilization is derived from the Latin term *civis*, which means citizen. Historically, not all inhabitants of a civilization were considered citizens and did not share the same rights and liberties. Although civilized societies originated thousands of years ago, participation in governance was reserved for the wealthy and the elite. Indeed, wealth could not be accumulated by those in the lower classes because they were either owned by or owed a duty of obedience to a master. A concentration of wealth and power persisted for thousands of years.

The city-state of Athens in the 5th century BC is among the oldest documented democracies; however, only 10% to 20% of the population were considered citizens and were eligible to participate in the democratic process. Citizenship was gender-biased and hereditary—only those males born to an Athenian father were considered citizens.

At about the same time and continuing for 500 years, the Roman Republic was established as a form of democracy as well. Romans received citizenship by birth, but they also naturalized new citizens and granted citizenship to freed slaves. Slavery was extensive and most slaves had no chance of advancement, but some who were educated and filled more administrative roles could achieve citizenship eventually. The Republic distributed power across the Senate, consuls, and representative assemblies.

The Roman Senate primarily consisted of wealthy aristocrats whose actions consistently favored the wealthy. Other citizens were granted a role in governance through several representative councils. They had the authority to vote on matters of war and elect magistrates, but they were stacked with the wealthiest members of the broader community.

The cautionary tale from the Roman Republic is that the structure encouraged leaders to build bases of power and coalitions to advance their political agendas, and the centralization of power among special interests ultimately made the government less democratic over time. Julius Caesar leveraged the power bases to accumulate power for himself and essentially engineered a coup from within the government. He secured powers that enabled him to expand the government, thereby diluting special interests and controlling a sufficient majority of senators. He then installed himself as dictator and ended the Republic.

The U.S. was the first nation to define itself based on the ideals of the Enlightenment, which were articulated by philosophers such as John Locke, Thomas Hobbes, and Jean-Jacques Rousseau. They believed that government should be a social contract grounded in natural rights with the consent of the governed. The separation of powers was modeled on the structure of the Roman Republic. The founding principles were noble, but it took over 100 years to transform the culture of the growing nation into one that applied them broadly and inclusively.

U.S. Citizenship and Voting

Neither the U.S. Constitution nor the Bill of Rights (Amendments I through X) defined citizenship. The federal government was not directly involved in determining or tracking citizenship from the founding of the U.S. until Congress passed the Naturalization Act of 1906 when it established the Bureau of Naturalization, standardized forms, and introduced central record-keeping. Previously, any court could issue a naturalization certificate, and there was a significant risk of loss and fraud. The federal government became significantly more involved in the administration and oversight of both immigration and naturalization in 1933 with the establishment and funding of the Immigration and Naturalization Service.

The founding documents, up to and including the Bill of Rights, did not define who has the right to vote and left that determination and the process to the states, except for states presenting Electoral College votes to the U.S. Congress in the election of the president and vice president. Many states allowed non-citizens to vote until the 1920s, provided they declared their intent to become citizens, and federal law did not explicitly prohibit non-citizen voting until 1996. The election process in the U.S., whether for federal or state office, is and has always been conducted by the states. Therefore, individual state action or inaction can significantly affect Americans' ability to participate fully in the democratic process. The right to vote was addressed in five Constitutional amendments:

- The 15th Amendment, ratified in 1870, established that the right to vote could not be denied on account of race, color, or previous condition of servitude.
- The 19th Amendment, ratified in 1920, established that the right to vote could not be denied on account of sex, guaranteeing women the right to vote.

- The 23rd Amendment, ratified in 1961, extended the right to vote in presidential elections to residents of the District of Columbia.
- The 24th Amendment, ratified in 1964, established that the right to vote could not be denied for failure to pay a poll tax or any other tax (five states still required a poll tax at the time).
- The 26th Amendment, ratified in 1971, established that the right to vote could not be denied on account of age for any citizen 18 years of age or older.

With these amendments, citizenship in the U.S. comes with the right to vote for anyone age 18 or older, which is the foundation of shared self-governance. Our challenge as a culture is that, while we enable broad participation in our democracy, just over half of the eligible population votes in presidential elections, and fewer than one-third participate in all other elections. That is the lowest rate among developed nations with democratic institutions.

Challenges with the Way Forward

The U.S. will not achieve its ideals unless more eligible voters participate in the voting process, and that requires better civic education and diligence to thwart activities that suppress the vote. People who participate in governance tend to shape institutions to meet their needs. We need only look at the post-Reconstruction era to see that when newly emancipated Black Americans were excluded from voting and representation, laws were passed that limited their rights and thus gave a disproportionate advantage to those able to participate in the democratic process. If certain voices are being suppressed or otherwise not heard, then the institutions fail to reflect the needs of the broader population.

Alternatively, when those with wealth are allowed to amplify their voices because they control corporations that have been granted human rights, the system becomes corrupted. Successful shared self-governance requires that everyone has an equal voice and the opportunity to be heard. The Supreme Court must reverse its Citizens United decision that has allowed corporate money to pour into elections. Corporate influence also shapes the legislative process through the lobbying industry. When citizens engage, they should not have to overcome the disproportionate influence and financial resources of corporate interests.

The two seemingly irreconcilable viewpoints described in the introduction—those who want to share the wealth with those less fortunate and those who do not—are today in an electoral fight for control of government institutions and the policy-making apparatus. Very much like the height of Jim Crow South, the modern faction that wants to exclude others from full participation in society and the economy is manipulating the tools of government to accomplish their selfish goals. The structure of the U.S. federal government can be leveraged to achieve a different outcome, but only if a majority of people participating in the democratic process push for it.

9

Population Health and Well-Being

Concentrations of wealth and poverty have perpetuated barriers to Black and Native Americans and immigrants from fully participating in the economy and society. Sharing wealth is not an end in itself, but it is also critical for enabling people to enjoy a reasonable standard of living and a high quality of life. While programs were enacted in President Lyndon Johnson's *War on Poverty* in the 1960s and the decades since, funding for them is threatened in almost every session of Congress.

In 1948, the United Nations (U.N.) adopted the Universal Declaration of Human Rights (UDHR). It was drafted by the 18-person U.N. Commission on Human Rights, which was chaired by FDR's widow, Eleanor Roosevelt. While it was not binding, the document represented the collective conscience of the world in its effort to prevent the atrocities of World War II from happening again. It also enshrined values that were relatively new across the span of human history and not universally guaranteed, as many descendants from slaves in the U.S. and several other former slave-holding countries continued to struggle with discrimination and barriers to full participation in their economies and societies.

The UDHR was remarkable for its visionary approach, which went beyond the practices of many countries at the time. Many of the rights enshrined in the document have been committed in writing through treaties among member nations, though not all treaties have been universally accepted. While Americans enjoy many of the rights in the UDHR, one commitment stands out as unfulfilled. Article 25 states that:

> *"Everyone has the right to a standard of living adequate for the health and well-being of himself and of his family, including food, clothing, housing and medical care and necessary social services, and the right to security in the event of unemployment, sickness, disability, widowhood, old age or other lack of livelihood in circumstances beyond his control."*[15]

The U.S. government does not currently acknowledge a right to any of the elements in Article 25, although some programs have been developed to provide support in certain areas. This chapter is vital because income and wealth disparities, as well as their drivers, also contribute to health disparities.

It is notable that the U.S. has signed but not ratified the International Covenant on Economic, Social, and Cultural Rights (ICESCR), a U.N. treaty adopted in 1966 and entered into force in 1976; 173 U.N. member countries have fully ratified it. The rights articulated in the document include those in Article 25 of the UDHR, as well as rights to (1) primary, secondary, and higher education, (2) work in safe conditions with fair wages and appropriate leisure time, and

---

[15] https://www.un.org/en/about-us/universal-declaration-of-human-rights

(3) environmental protection (written as "environmental and industrial hygiene").

The rights granted by the ICESCR are the very rights that American culture resists sharing broadly, in part because of the financial commitment required and in part because the culture still harbors deep-seated, unstated biases against full equality that have persisted for centuries.

Health in the Early 20th Century

By the start of the 20th century, the Industrial Revolution had created numerous circumstances that negatively affected the health and well-being of workers. Working families endured significant financial stress, often with all family members, including young children, working to generate sufficient income to survive. Living conditions were cramped and unsanitary, and nutrition was poor due to limited resources and inadequate health knowledge. Workplaces were often hazardous, and workers were expected to work long hours, typically 11-12 hours per day.

People were broadly vulnerable to illness and death because the medical profession was in its infancy. Primary care was available on a fee-for-service basis from general practitioners; however, these services were only accessible to those who were wealthy enough to afford the fees. Charitable hospitals, often affiliated with religious institutions, were established to serve the working poor. Some workers gained access to healthcare through their employers or labor unions, while others gained it through mutual benefit societies. Access to healthcare, though, was not as broad as it is today.

The Medicaid and Medicare programs, created during President Lyndon Johnson's *War on Poverty*, play a significant role in mitigating the impact of poverty on health. While they help cover the cost of health services, they have a less direct effect on access to care. To be sure, healthcare delivery in some rural and impoverished areas would not exist without the support of these funding sources for otherwise uninsured residents; however, a payment mechanism alone is insufficient. People living in poverty have fewer healthcare resources available to them than most others.

Modern American Healthcare

In concept, the U.S. should have the best health outcomes across the entire population because it is the wealthiest country in the world. Americans spend approximately $4 trillion on healthcare annually, accounting for around 18% of the country's GDP—a rate higher than that of any other developed country since 1981. The higher cost is not driving better outcomes; Americans, on average, are less healthy than people in other developed countries.

The Organization for Economic Cooperation and Development (OECD) publishes extensive data about its 38 member countries. The U.S. has the highest rates of infant and maternal mortality, obesity, and chronic disease and falls in the bottom 10 countries for life expectancy. The 21 highest-income countries in the OECD that outperform the U.S. on every health measure have universal healthcare systems and spend a much lower percentage of their GDP on healthcare.

The discussion in Chapters 3 and 4 focused on the vast income and wealth disparities in the U.S. Countries with wide income and wealth disparities tend to have poorer health outcomes than those with narrower income and wealth disparities. Dozens of higher-income countries provide universal healthcare, which helps to ensure better overall health.

People living in poverty in the U.S. often have poorer health outcomes and higher rates of chronic diseases than the rest of the population. Healthy food and healthcare are less accessible and more expensive in communities with concentrations of poverty created by the discriminatory housing policies in the mid-20th century. Workers and their families who struggle with poverty have more stress about personal safety, making ends meet, and the impact of potential job loss. Stress makes people more susceptible to illnesses, including chronic diseases, which reduce productivity and increase costs.

Economic Considerations

According to data from the U.S. Centers for Disease Control (CDC), treatment for chronic disease and mental health conditions accounts for 90% of healthcare costs.[16] There is a much higher incidence of chronic and mental health conditions among people living in poverty. Consigning people to poverty and then withholding healthcare comes at a significant cost.

---

[16] https://www.cdc.gov/chronic-disease/data-research/facts-stats/index.html#cdc_facts_stats_intro-the-impact-of-chronic-diseases-in-america

While the healthcare industry may profit from treating chronic conditions, these conditions are often caused and exacerbated by activities that benefit other sectors. Smoking, poor nutrition, physical inactivity, and excessive alcohol consumption are significant contributors to chronic disease. An economy driven by an unconstrained free market can thus thrive even though people are unhealthy.

Employees struggling with health problems are less productive. The level of chronic illness in the U.S. far outstrips other developed economies and drives up the cost of doing business. Universal healthcare that promotes wellness could help reduce the high cost of healthcare, although some corporate and business interests may suffer if the industry shrinks due to less demand.

Economic and business interests lobby for legislation and fund parties or candidates that support their profitability, which is a significant barrier to reform. Granting speech rights to corporations enables the wealthy elite who control them to amplify their voices and exert greater influence.

There are more localized economic impacts that, in aggregate, harm the overall economy. Without universal healthcare, individual patients and their families are exposed to crushing medical debt. Personal bankruptcies can have a generational toll on families, and as many as 50% to 60% result from medical debt. Beyond the impact on families, these ultimately increase costs for businesses that are forced to write off debts, driving down profitability.

Health Policy Recommendations

Wealth, poverty, and health are interconnected. The commitments made in the UDHR were novel when they were articulated in 1948, but now, more than 70 years later, they are common sense. The U.S. should stand up against corporate power to defend safety-net programs and enact universal healthcare legislation, which not only protects rights acknowledged by many other developed countries worldwide but can also bolster parts of the U.S. economy that are burdened by the cost of an expensive and ineffective approach to healthcare.

CONCLUSION

The U.S. is a nation struggling with its identity. One large segment of society embraces diversity and seeks to overcome the inequities that resulted from centuries of discrimination against non-white people. Another sizable, primarily white, segment questions the value of diversity and fights efforts to acknowledge or overcome past discrimination, seemingly because they choose not to see the advantages they have in our current economy. There is a historical foundation for this tension, and this book was written to remind us of that history and show how our institutions have been skewed to work to the advantage of an elite few at the disadvantage of a significant portion of the U.S. population. We must strengthen and work within the institutions established under the Constitution to overcome the disparities that have prevented the U.S. from achieving the ideals it shared with the majority of countries worldwide when it drafted and signed the United Nations Declaration of Human Rights shortly after the conclusion of World War II.

In Chapter 1, we discussed how European monarchs and nations battled for supremacy across the world. European exploration led to the colonization and exploitation of most of the Americas and Caribbean Islands, with a significant toll on the Indigenous populations. As the North American colonies developed, violence erupted between settlers and Native Americans, as well as among settlers from different countries of origin. The colonists persisted, expanded their presence, and established a robust economy designed to enrich the European colonists and their descendants, ostensibly at the expense of Native Americans and enslaved Africans—but that part of the history is often suppressed.

Chapter 2 shifted to how the U.S. evolved since its founding, expanding west to encompass a large portion of the North American continent. The expansion was initiated by paying or negotiating with other powers for territorial control, but it was ultimately accomplished through violence and dispossession. Much of the chapter focused on the divisive impact of slavery and its aftermath, including another century of explicit discrimination to limit the full participation of Black Americans in society and the economy.

Chapter 3 described how the unconstrained free-market economy during the Industrial Revolution led to wide income and wealth disparities. It also discussed how those disparities narrowed during the period following the Great Depression due in large part to New Deal programs implemented in the 1930s. As the U.S. entered the 1980s, tax policy and economic factors resulted in widening disparities that have persisted and worsened over the subsequent four decades.

Leveraging research released in the past decade, Chapter 4 explained the factors that result in persistent poverty and those that perpetuate wealth across generations. The housing policy that created concentrations of poverty imposed on Black Americans established the conditions that resulted in persistent disadvantage. The chapter also provided an analysis showing that taxes paid by high-income families and benefits received by lower-income families narrowed but did not erase the growth in income disparities over the past several decades.

The modern U.S. individual income tax system, discussed in Chapter 5, was designed to combat some of the early disparities by taxing those who most benefit economically from the system of government to support its cost. Although special interests intervened throughout the life of the tax code, it remained highly progressive for more than 70 years, adhering to the ideals of economic fairness on which it was founded. Following a drastic restructuring of the tax code, people today focus on making incremental changes to the current structure rather than revisiting and restoring the structures that were more equitable in the past. Coupled with economic forces that coincided with major tax reform, the U.S. has ended with a working class earning stagnant wages that are insufficient to sustain a family and a significant skew of financial outcomes and power toward the wealthiest households.

Labor practices that affect the working class were discussed in Chapter 6. The working classes were excluded from full participation in society and the economy for thousands of years until the Enlightenment in the 18th century. As the Industrial Revolution created opportunities for workers to exercise autonomy, they also needed protection from an economic framework that gave too much power to owners and managers, who underpaid workers, demanded unreasonable work hours, and ignored worker safety. Labor laws guaranteeing workers' rights to collective bargaining and representation, setting a minimum wage and establishing standard work hours were critical to address the imbalance of power and economic inequity. Still, the federal minimum wage no longer allows a worker to support a family with a single full-time job.

The Industrial Revolution gave rise to numerous capital-intensive businesses that were best suited to a corporate structure due to their ability to raise funds from multiple investors. In Chapter 7, we discussed their origin and the significant growth in the number and size of corporations during the 19th century. This legal structure enabled companies to scale significantly, expanding employment and driving economic growth. However, corporate income tax rates in the U.S. have long been lower than individual income tax rates. In recent years, efforts to pare them further have limited the resources generated by the corporate tax.

The opportunity for broad, shared self-governance that we have today has only been available anywhere in the world for a few hundred years, as described in Chapter 8. We have the power to influence the policies that guide the nation's development through our active participation in democracy. Still, the U.S. falls short of participation levels seen in other developed countries. The factions that benefit from the status quo engage in efforts to limit and discourage participation. More voter engagement is needed to counter the threats to the progress that the U.S. has made in recent years.

As discussed in Chapter 9, while the U.S. was still denying Black Americans full participation in the economy and society in the 1940s, the U.N. Human Rights Commission codified rights that were to be universally applied without regard to race, gender, or several other criteria. Unlike 173 other U.N.

member countries, the U.S. has not ratified a treaty that would acknowledge rights to food, housing, and medical care, among others, that are being withheld due to a lack of political will to address the nation's struggle to share the wealth. Most other developed countries have some form of universal healthcare, and they achieve better health outcomes at a lower cost, as a percentage of GDP, than does the U.S.

The Industrial Revolution transformed the world and altered the way people interacted with one another. Unconstrained corporate behavior and the resulting channeling of economic rewards to an elite few required government action to create a more equitable society. There were two eras of significant progress: immediately following the Great Depression and the 1960s, when civil rights and concern for those living in poverty sparked innovation in public programs.

The choices made by more recent generations have created a significant disparity in the U.S. between those with and without advantages, which affects the overall health and prosperity of our nation compared to other developed countries. Cultures around the world have embraced more broadly inclusive rights than the U.S., and many have made progress in protecting them. While the U.S. economy remains the largest, it is no longer a land of equal opportunity for those pursuing the American Dream.

While there is inconsistent data to correlate pervasive poverty with overall economic growth, it is plausible that lifting people out of poverty will drive consumer spending. The expanded child tax credit, which was in place in 2021, coincided with strong consumer spending, fueling growth and profitability that outstripped other countries climbing out of the COVID crisis. Even if the wealthy do not agree that others deserve a more level playing field, it can be economically beneficial to share the wealth more.

Throughout human history, civilizations that collapse due to internal rather than external factors often do so under the weight of domestic strife. An economically polarized society is not sustainable. It is a short-term strategy to hoard wealth at the expense of others; people smart enough to manipulate the system to their advantage should recognize this.

In the Introduction, I stated that it is unjust for people to live in poverty in a country of immense wealth. Indeed, dozens of other developed nations have done a better job than the U.S. at limiting poverty. We have allowed our system of shared self-governance to be corrupted by the greed of a small minority, who pit the middle class against the working class under the guise of scarcity while working behind the scenes to get an increasing share of the true abundance in our world. Past efforts to work toward a more egalitarian society created the middle class; we now need to reclaim the levers of government to complete the work and lift the rest of Americans out of poverty.

Here are some steps readers can take to support this goal:

- Advocate for tax reform that adds tax brackets above the current structure. Billionaires and multi-millionaires should not be subject to the same low marginal tax rate as the middle or upper-middle class; instead, income for the middle class should fall within the middle of the tax rate schedule.

- Advocate for tax reform that does not give significant economic advantage to corporations that the owners and leaders then use to lobby for their interests at the expense of the rest of us.
- Advocate to retain and strengthen social safety net programs to protect the vulnerable while doing the work to reduce dependence on the programs, which should be funded by higher taxes on the rich and corporations that have benefited most from low worker wages.
- Advocate for a higher federal minimum wage of at least $15 per hour to lift millions of people out of poverty, reducing dependence on safety net programs.
- Advocate for universal healthcare and healthcare reform to reduce exorbitant costs that all Americans bear.

If you are in the middle or upper-middle class, what do you have to lose by advocating for these changes? I do not see much to sacrifice—but a significant amount to gain.

Lifting people out of poverty will:

- Expand business opportunities to sell to a growing population with disposable income.
- Reduce blight and raise property values by enabling more Americans to invest in their own homes.
- Reduce the incidence of chronic disease by enabling people to afford better nutrition and preventive care. Lowered levels of disease will lower the cost for everyone.

Following the lead of dozens of other nations, universal healthcare will eliminate the risk that we are all just one severe illness or injury away from bankruptcy. More accessible care will result in fewer people turning to emergency rooms for primary care, making them more effective for everyone. Improved health will increase worker productivity, driving economic growth.

Despite the tremendous growth we have experienced in the U.S., considerable tension remains between segments of our society. Some in power suggest that we are competing for scarce resources, but the data does not support this claim. The U.S. has created significant wealth; in the end, however, it has not been distributed equitably.

BIBLIOGRAPHY

On the colonial period:

- William John Eccles, *Seven Years' War*, Canadian Encyclopedia, 2/7/2006. https://www.thecanadianencyclopedia.ca/en/article/seven-years-war
- Bill of Rights Institute. *Essay: Native Americans*. https://billofrightsinstitute.org/essays/native-americans/
- Robert M Kozub, *Antecedents of the income tax in colonial America*, Accounting Historians Journal: Volume 10: Issue 2, Article 7, 1983. https://egrove.olemiss.edu/aah_journal/vol10/iss2/7
- David Wheat and Ida Altman, *The seventeenth-century Spanish Caribbean as global crossroads: transimperial and transregional approaches*, Colonial Latin American Review, 32(1), 1–10, (2023). https://doi.org/10.1080/10609164.2023.2170549

On the economic impact of government policy:

- Kevin Phillips, *The Politics of Rich and Poor: Wealth and the American Electorate in the Reagan Aftermath*, HarperCollins Publishers, New York, NY, 1990.
- Ajay Chaudry, Christopher Wimer, Suzanne Macartney, Lauren Frohlich, Colin Campbell, Kendal Swenson, Don Oellerich, and Susan Hauan, *Poverty in the United States: 50-Year Trends and Safety Net Impacts, Office of Human Services Policy*, U.S. Department of Health and Human Services, March 2016.
- Erick Corimanya, *The Free Market Myth: Unveiling the Illusions of Economic Justice*, New Angle Press, 2025.
- Phil Gramm, Robert Ekelund, & John Early, The *Myth of American Inequality: How Government Biases Policy Debate,* Rowman & Littlefield, 2022.
- Timothy Vermeer, Alex Durante, Erica York, Jared Walczak, America's *Progressive Tax and Transfer System: Federal, State, and Local Tax and Transfer Distributions*, Tax Foundation, 2023. https://taxfoundation.org/research/all/federal/who-pays-taxes-federal-state-local-tax-burden-transfers/
- Brynne Keith-Jennings and Raheem Chaudhry, *Most Working-Age SNAP Participants Work, But Often in Unstable Jobs*, Center on Budget and Policy Priorities, 2018. https://www.cbpp.org/research/most-working-age-snap-participants-work-but-often-in-unstable-jobs

On racial justice:

- Dorothy A. Brown, *The Whiteness of Wealth: How the Tax System Impoverishes Black Americans—and How We Can Fix It*, Penguin RandomHouse, New York, NY, 2021.
- Isabel Wilkerson, *Caste: The Origins of Our Discontents*, Penguin Random House, New York, NY, 2023.
- Diana Elliott, *Two American Experiences: The Racial Divide of Poverty*, Urban Institute, Urban Wire blog, July 16, 2016.
- Abhay Aneja and Guo Xu, *The Costs of Employment Segregation: Evidence from the Federal Government Under Woodrow Wilson*, National Bureau of Economic Research, 2021.

On the depth and persistence of poverty:

- Eric Dearing, Andres S. Bustamante, Henrik D. Zachrisson, & Deborah Lowe Vandell, *Accumulation of Opportunities Predicts the Educational Attainment and Adulthood Earnings of Children Born Into Low- Versus Higher-Income Households*. Educational Researcher, 53(9), 496-507, 2024. https://doi.org/10.3102/0013189X241283456
- David Brady, *Poverty, not the poor*, Science Advances, Volume 9, Issue 34, August 2023.
- Mathew Desmond, *Poverty, by America*, Penguin Random House, 2023.

- Eugene Smolensky and Robert Plotnick, *Inequality and Poverty in the United States: 1900 to 1990*, Institute for Research on Poverty, University of Madison-Wisconsin, 1993.
- Edward N. Wolf, *Household Wealth Trends in the United States, 1962 to 2019: Median Wealth Rebounds... But Not Enough*, National Bureau of Economic Research, 2021.
- John Iceland, *Poverty in America: A Handbook*, Third Edition, University of California Press, 2013.

On the practice of redlining:

- Richard Rothstein, *The Color of Law: A Forgotten History of How Our Government Segregated America*, Liveright Publishing, New York, NY, 2017.
- Daniel Aaronson, Daniel Hartley, & Bhashkar Mazumder. (2021). *The effects of the 1930s HOLC "redlining" maps*, American Economic Journal: Economic Policy, American Economic Association, vol. 13(4), pages 355-392, November.
- Robert K. Nelson, LaDale Winling, Todd Michney, et al., *Mapping inequality: Redlining in New Deal America*, Digital Scholarship Lab, University of Richmond, 2020.
  https://dsl.richmond.edu/panorama/redlining
- Dylan Lukes and Christopher Cleveland, *The Lingering Legacy of Redlining on School Funding, Diversity, and Performance*. (EdWorkingPaper: 21-363). Retrieved from Annenberg Institute at Brown University, 2021:
  https://doi.org/10.26300/qeer-8c25

On the history of taxation and corporations:

- Alvin Rabushka, *The Colonial Roots of American Taxation, 1607-1700*, Hoover Institution, 2002. https://www.hoover.org/research/colonial-roots-american-taxation-1607-1700
- Emmanuel Saez, *Striking it Richer: The Evolution of Top Incomes in the United States*, University of California—Berkley, 2015.
- Thomas L. Hungerford, *U.S. Federal Government Revenues: 1790 to the Present*, Congressional Research Service, 2006.
- *Legal Status of Capital Gains*, Joint Committee on Internal Revenue Taxation, 1959.
- Ralph Edward Gomory and Richard Sylla, *The American Corporation*, Daedalus, the Journal of the American Academy Spring 2013 Issue, pp. 102-118. https://www.amacad.org/publication/daedalus/american-corporation

On wealth:

- Fabian T Pfeffer and Alexandra Killewald, *Generations of Advantage. Multigenerational Correlations in Family Wealth*, Social Forces, Volume 96, Issue 4, June 2018, Pages 1411–1442. https://doi.org/10.1093/sf/sox086

- Philipp Ager, Leah Boustan and Katherine Eriksson, *The Intergenerational Effects of a Large Wealth Shock: White Southerners after the Civil War*, American Economic Review 2021, 111(11): 3767–3794.
- Raj Chetty, Nathaniel Hendren, Patrick Kline, & Emmanuel Saez, *Where is the land of opportunity? The geography of intergenerational mobility in the United States*. Quarterly Journal of Economics, 129(4), 1553–1623, 2014. https://doi.org/10.1093/qje/qju022
- Fabian T. Pfeffer, Alexandra & Killewald, *Generations of advantage: Multigenerational correlations in family wealth*. Social Forces, 96(4): 1411–1442, 2018. https://doi.org/10.1093/sf/sox086
- Thomas Piketty, *Capital in the Twenty-First Century*, Harvard University Press, 2014.
- Thomas M. Shapiro, *The hidden cost of being African American: How wealth perpetuates inequality*, Oxford University Press, 2004.

General data sources:

- SOI Tax Stats - Individual income tax return and SOI tax stats - Corporation tax statistics. https://www.irs.gov/statistics/soi-tax-stats-individual-income-tax-return-form-1040-statistics
- Scott Hollenbeck and Maureen Keenan Kahr, *Ninety Years of Individual Income and Tax Statistics, 1916-2005*, Internal Revenue Service, 2008.

- David Paris and Cecelia Hilgert, *70th Year of Individual Income and Tax Statistics, 1913-1982*, Internal Revenue Service, 1984.
- Title: *National Income and Product Accounts of the United States, 1929-97*, Volume 1.

  Table 1.1.—Gross Domestic Product: Annually, 1929-97.

  Table 5.1.—Gross Saving and Investment: Annually, 1929-97.

  Table 1.14.—National Income by Type of Income: Annually, 1929-97.

  https://fraser.stlouisfed.org/title/national-income-product-accounts-benchmark-revisions-181/national-income-product-accounts-united-states-1929-97-5416?page=143

ABOUT THE AUTHOR

After a 40-year career spanning roles in professional services, corporate marketing and finance, and the nonprofit sector, Michael has shifted his focus to consulting and writing. This book emerged from the intersection of Michael's work with marginalized communities and his technical background in accounting and tax.

Michael attended Georgetown Day School, the first integrated school in the District of Columbia, and then the Jesuit-led Georgetown University, where he earned a Bachelor of Science degree in Business Administration. While both institutions are known for their commitment to social justice, he learned most about the impact of America's imperfect history on disadvantaged populations through his work in the nonprofit sector. He also spent some of his years in the public accounting field working on tax compliance for individuals and corporations.

Michael D. Ward

While Michael was involved in nonprofit accounting as early as the mid-1980s, his substantive nonprofit experience began when served as the Chief Financial Officer of the Lt. Joseph P. Kennedy Institute from 1998 to 2001 and then as its President and Chief Executive Officer from 2001 to 2004. From that point forward, he has provided professional services to nonprofit organizations and small to medium sized businesses through his work with three accounting firms, culminating in over eight years as a Partner/Principal with BDO USA.

Prior to his work with Kennedy Institute, he worked in the audit practices of two Big-8 accounting firms in the 1980s and early 1990s, served as a Controller for two privately owned companies. and spent over five years in strategic finance roles in the Consumer Markets division of MCI Telecommunications, working on airline partnerships, an internal loyalty program, 1-800 MUSIC NOW, 1-800-COLLECT, and 10-10-321.

www.ingramcontent.com/pod-product-compliance
Lightning Source LLC
Chambersburg PA
CBHW060502030426
42337CB00015B/1691